Duke University

THE CAMPUS GUIDE

Duke University

An Architectural Tour by
John M. Bryan
Photographs by Robert C. Lautman
Foreword by Tallman Trask III

Princeton Architectural Press
NEW YORK | 2000

This book has been made possible through the generous support
of the Graham Foundation for Advanced Studies in the Fine Arts.

All black-and-white photographs are generously provided by and
in the collection of Duke University Archives.

Princeton Architectural Press
37 East 7th Street
New York, NY 10003
212.995.9620

For a free catalog of other books published by Princeton Architectural Press,
call toll free 1.800.722.6657 or visit our web site at www.papress.com

Series editor: Jan Cigliano
Copy editor: Heather Ewing
Design: Sara Stemen
Layout: Mary-Neal Meador
Maps: Jane Garvie
Special thanks to Ann Alter, Amanda Atkins, Nicola Bednarek, Eugenia Bell, Caroline
Green, Beth Harrison, Mia Ihara, Clare Jacobson, Leslie Ann Kent, Mark Lamster,
Anne Nitschke, Lottchen Shivers, Jennifer Thompson, and Deb Wood of Princeton
Architectural Press
—Kevin C. Lippert, *publisher*

Library of Congress Cataloguing-in-Publication Data
Bryan, John Morrill.
     Duke University : an architectural tour / by John M. Bryan ; photographs by Robert
C. Lautman ; foreword by Tallman Trask III.
          p. cm. (The campus guide)
Includes bibliographical references and index.
ISBN 1-56898-228-3
1. Duke University—Buildings—Guidebooks. I. Title. II. Campus guide (New York,
N.Y.)
LD1732.D8323 B79 2000
378.756 563˙DC21   00-044612
                                                              CIP

Printed in China
04 03 02 01 00   5 4 3 2 1

How to use this book

This guide is intended for visitors, alumni, and students who wish to have an insider's look at the most historic and interesting buildings, gardens, and quadrangles on Duke University's campus, from the Chapel and the Gothic style West Campus, to the Washington Duke Building and the Georgian style East Campus, to the Sarah P. Duke Gardens, Duke University Museum of Art, Wade Stadium, and Krzyzewskiville Tent Plaza.

The book is divided into seven Walks. Each Walk covers a specific area of the campus and opens with a three-dimensional aerial map that locates the buildings on the walk. Following an introductory essay of the area, the major buildings on the walk are illustrated with color photographs and historical and architectural profiles.

Campus buildings open: 8:30AM to 5PM Monday–Saturday, year-round

Duke University Museum of Art open: 10AM to 5PM Tuesday–Friday, 10AM to 9PM Wednesday, 11AM to 2PM Saturday, 2PM to 5PM Sunday. Free admission; donations accepted. East Campus. Parking available behind museum.

Duke Chapel open: dawn–dusk year-round, except Christmas day; prayer services 5:15PM Tuesday and Wednesday, 11AM Sunday, 9PM Sunday; carillon recital 5PM Monday–Friday; organ music 12:30PM Monday–Tuesday and Thursday–Friday; choral concert 12PM Wednesday and 4PM Sunday. 919.684.2572

Sarah P. Duke Gardens open: 8AM–dusk, year-round. Free admission. 919.684.3698

Botany Greenhouse open: 10AM–4:30PM Monday–Thursday. 919.660.7334

Primate Center tours: 8:30AM–5PM Monday–Friday, 8:30AM–1PM Saturday. By appointment only. Admission: $6 adults, $3 seniors, $4 college students, $3 children 3–12 years. Located on the edge of Duke Forest. 919.489.3364

Duke University Stores open: 8:30AM–5PM Monday–Saturday, year-round. 800.842.3853 or 919.684.2065

Duke Athletics, Cameron Indoor Stadium: 919.684.2431

Further information:

Duke University
Office of Public Information
Durham, North Carolina 27708
919.684.3214
fax 919.681.8941
www.duke.edu
askduke@admiss.duke.edu

Foreword

Crowell Quadrangle

Upon hearing that Trinity College would become Duke University in 1924, a disgruntled alumnus wrote: "Nothing short of a miracle can ever establish a truly great university in a place like Durham." Tobacco baron James Buchanan Duke had just signed the indenture that would launch the small school on its path to prominence, with facilities and reputation to match. At that time, neither our West Campus nor its 210-foot-high Duke Chapel existed; neither did the business, medical, engineering, or divinity schools. East Campus was a smattering of buildings housing all of 180 students who must have looked around themselves and blinked, wondering if they were dreaming.

Duke University literally grew up with the last three-quarters of the twentieth century, coming into full flower along with its home city. Few could have foreseen the transformation from the struggling college, located on a former racetrack, into one of the world's top teaching and research institutions.

When students look back on their college experience, particularly their undergraduate experience, their memories are apt to be tied to places. A cornice can evoke a whole discussion on Platonic philosophers; a particular nicked dentil may overwhelm one with the memory of a kiss received nearby.

D. H. Lawrence, in his essay "The Spirit of Place," wrote,

> Different places on the face of the earth have different vital effluence, different vibration, different chemical exhalation, different polarity with different stars: call it what you like. But the spirit of place is a great reality. The Nile Valley produced not only the corn, but the terrific religions of Egypt.

Place signifies. Architecturally as well as academically, Duke University had nothing if not "outrageous ambition," as former president Terry Sanford said. While at the outset many (Northerners) argued that the South could never spawn a truly great university, today others suggest that Duke in fact became a great university in part because it *looked* like one from the start. J. B. Duke himself wanted it this way, and he spent not only much money but much personal time on the original plans, worrying about everything from architectural detail and landscaping, to whether there should be "less of the yellow and gold colors" in the stone mix. (Just last week we had the same conversation with the architect for a new dormitory, reassuring us that there is a certain consistency to life.)

In 1931 President William Preston Few told the graduating class, "These buildings have been constructed . . . to be the home of the soul of the University and in the belief that these appropriate and beautiful surroundings will have a transforming influence upon students generation after generation and even upon the character of the institution itself."[1]

He hoped the buildings would remind those who worked and studied here of their high mission to nurture *eruditio et religio* while defining a sense of place that fostered camaraderie, spiritual and intellectual growth, a sense of infinite possibility, and infinite yearning. At the same time, the grotesques and gargoyles that grace the facades, rooftops, and entryways of West Campus—many of which seem to represent priggish professors—were to keep us from taking ourselves too seriously. Renaissance architects had talked openly about how buildings could shape the souls of people in them. These no-nonsense industrialists believed it, and acted on that belief.

Aldous Huxley, writing in 1937, described a trip through the pine forests of North Carolina, a land "where one would never expect anything in particular to happen. And then, all of a sudden, something does happen. . . . There, astonishingly, is by far the largest Gothic building one has ever seen. The eye wanders in amazement," he continued, "over a whole city of grey stone. . . . These buildings are genuinely beautiful . . . [f]or this huge and fantastic structure which houses a large university . . . is the most successful essay in neo-Gothic that I know."[2]

It is one of the great ironies of our brief institutional history—and perhaps an odd tribute to the farsightedness of our founders—that the practical dreamer behind most of the campus, a man whose relationship with Duke University lasted nearly a quarter century and whose portrait sits just inside the entrance of our administration building, could not have gained admission during his lifetime because he was black. What Few and Huxley acknowledged with astonishment and humility was largely the product of the mind of Julian F. Abele, chief designer for the architectural firm of Horace Trumbauer in Philadelphia. So far as we know, Abele never visited his creation at first hand, deterred from travel by the South's Jim Crow laws.

Be that as it may, his masterpiece would remain, from his point of view, a virtual project through his death in 1950, visible in his mind's eye and in the magnificent drawings he left, grand in scale and exquisite in detail. One of the last buildings he designed, and one of the few with his name alone on the drawings, was Cameron Indoor Stadium, a shrine of college basketball and a symbol of one of the few American universities that has remained consistently superb academically, and athletically.

The unity of Abele's vision was itself rooted in Eurocentric history and his training in Paris. On East Campus, the flatness of the land and the style of the existing Trinity College buildings made Georgian architecture a sensible choice. Baldwin Auditorium still stands as a crown jewel in that coherent assemblage. On West Campus, of course, Gothic architecture was to prevail, but a Gothic updated and intelligently modernized, where it underscored ties with Old World knowledge while demonstrating with élan that Duke University would give the world something quite new as well.

We're proud to preserve it, display it, and honor it. May this book give you some sense of the spirit of this place.

Tallman Trask III
Executive Vice President
Duke University

1.   "Duke University Architecture Discussed by President W. P. Few," in *The [Duke University] Alumni Register* (June 1931): 195–97.
2.   Reprinted from *Time and Tide* in *Duke Alumni Register* (September 1937): 238.

The creation of Duke University is one of the dramatic stories in American educational and architectural history. To honor and expand a philanthropic tradition begun by his father, James B. Duke established the $40 million Duke Endowment in 1924. In creating the endowment he specified a variety of charitable beneficiaries, with the largest share (thirty-two percent) being allocated to transform a small, Methodist-affiliated college into a full-fledged research university. Two campuses—the Georgian style East Campus and the Gothic style West Campus—a hospital, twelve residences, and athletic facilities, all in total containing more than 23,287,000 cubic feet and costing approximately $22 million, were begun in 1925 and in operation by 1930.

Washington Duke

The Philadelphia architectural firm of Horace Trumbauer, with Julian F. Abele as principal designer, created the original buildings. The Olmsted Brothers of Brookline, Massachusetts, developed the landscape plan. The character of the two historic campuses stems from clearly articulated goals, ample funding, and a concentrated burst of construction directed by a few like-minded people.

After opening in 1930, Duke grew little for twenty years. But following World War II, changes in medicine, science, and in the professional schools created a pressure for growth that has accelerated in recent years. The new buildings reflect attempts to balance compatibility with a revered setting against changes in education, transportation, and construction costs and techniques. East Campus, framed by a wall

James Buchanan Duke (seated) and Benjamin Newton Duke

and a grid of city streets, has been relatively unaffected by this growth, but the boundaries of the West Campus have been blurred, and today there are arguably five or six—instead of two—distinct Duke University campuses.

A visit suggests a number of architectural themes. From the outset the physical plant was shaped to evoke memory as a goad to excellence. Administrators named places, placed plaques, and put up crests and insignia to keep exemplary individuals and institutions in the foreground throughout the day. On the old campuses, it is interesting to note design elements that contribute meaning and a sense of place, and then, looking at newer buildings, to observe changes prompted by cost, space, and the centrifugal effect of increasingly independent areas of specialized study.

The historic campuses are pedestrian oriented and designed to provide almost complete facilities for living and working on site. The quadrangle—a shared open space, or outdoor room defined by buildings—is central to the communal character of both East and West campus. On the other hand, most of the post-World War II buildings are sited to accommodate cars and the possibility of contiguous expansion. With a few notable exceptions, most of the new construction has focused on isolated buildings rather than quadrangles, and the result along Science Road and Research Drive resembles a spacious, well-landscaped office park instead of a traditional American campus.

Everywhere at Duke we are aware of the high standard set by its creators. Speaking to the 1931 graduating class, President William Preston Few concluded his remarks to the outgoing students by reminding them of the contribution of their own campus, saying, "The architectural harmony and strength of the plant is intended to suggest unity and fullness of life." This is worth remembering while touring Duke.

General view of campus looking toward West Campus

Chapel, at the end of Chapel Drive

The pillared entrance to Duke University is one of the great vistas in America. Visitors round a circle, enter Chapel Drive, cross a dell, and ascend the slope toward West Campus with the 210-foot-tall tower of the Chapel rising ahead like an exclamation point. The architectural drama of this approach reflects the intention of James Buchanan Duke (1857–1925), who actively directed the creation of a setting to reinforce goals specified in the Duke Endowment, the $40 million trust he established in 1924 to create the university.

The Gothic style West Campus is memorable, and for many people it is the image of Duke. But to know the university, the visitor also must experience the Georgian style East Campus (where the earliest buildings are located), tour the facilities along Research and Science Drives, enter the medical complex maze, become aware of residential pockets and smaller departments and offices filling interstices between the major educational units, and perhaps stroll through the Sarah P. Duke gardens and visit the Primate Center in the Duke Forest.

Duke's facilities in Durham, North Carolina, occupy approximately 1,700 acres and 150 major buildings. This physical plant serves some 11,200 students, 1,500 faculty, and 20,000 staff. It is too large and complex to cover comfortably in one day. The visitor with limited time may elect to focus on a few highlights, walk to points of interest, and then drive to get a superficial sense of the whole.

The campus lends itself to the seven separate tours that follow. These routes present different aspects of Duke, but each bears evidence of an ongoing attempt to mesh settings and aspirations. Consequently, the Duke environment is—literally and figuratively—telling.

Creating Duke: A Nutshell History

Washington Duke (1820–1905), who established the family in the tobacco business, became a benefactor of Trinity College in 1890. His initial gift of $85,000 was critical in inducing the small, Methodist-affiliated college to relocate from a rural setting to Durham. Washington Duke's sons, Benjamin Duke (1855–1929) and James Buchanan Duke, followed his example, for they supported Trinity and then provided the means to transform it into a modern university committed to research as well as undergraduate education.

Chapel Tower and Administration Building

Research universities on the German model were established in America in the last quarter of the nineteenth century. William Preston Few (1867–1940) served as president of Trinity College, 1910–1924, and subsequently as president of the new Duke University from 1925 to 1940. He was a native of South Carolina, had done graduate work at Harvard, and was keenly aware that no research-oriented universities existed in the South. He wanted to move Trinity College toward the new model, and younger faculty members supported his plans to introduce seminars, to produce scholarly publications, and to add postgraduate professional training to the curriculum.

Few apparently began to share his hopes for Trinity with the Duke brothers as early as 1916. Both brothers continued to support improvements at Trinity, and in 1924 James Buchanan Duke, the family financier and creator of the American Tobacco Company, the British and American Tobacco Company, and Duke Power, executed the Duke Endowment. This $40 million trust made possible the creation of a new research university and transformed Trinity into a college for women within the new, larger whole.

Trinity College was located on what is now the East Campus of Duke University. President Few, James B. Duke, and others initially anticipated acquiring adjacent property and expanding the existing campus. Neighbors of the college, however, hoped for windfall profits and inflated property values. Few later recalled walking with his sons in the woods one day and realizing that undeveloped, rolling woodland could be purchased reasonably. A quiet campaign ensued, and the college bought approximately 8,000 acres, 1.25 miles to the west.

The development of separate campuses for men and women at Duke was conceptually similar to the creation of Radcliffe at Harvard and Barnard at Columbia, but the *physical* separation of the facilities at Duke was based on the cost of real estate.

Contents

Scrapbook, Table of Contents, Professor Frank Clyde Brown

Although the Duke Endowment was not yet official, by the spring of 1924 President Few began gathering information about campus planning. He and Professor Frank Clyde Brown, chairman of the English department, made a whirlwind trip (March 25–April 10, 1924) to inspect other campuses. Brown's annotated scrapbook, apparently begun on this trip and added to as

the Proposed Chapel

Scrapbook, University of Chicago Chapel with anonymous sketch, Professor Frank Clyde Brown

information was received, includes material on Harvard, the Massachusetts Institute of Technology, Boston University, Bryn Mawr, the University of Chicago, the College of the City of New York, New York University, Columbia University, Cornell, Haverford, Johns Hopkins, Mount Holyoke, Peabody, Princeton, the University of Pennsylvania, Randolph Macon Womans College, Sweet Briar College, Syracuse University, Vassar, the University of Virginia, and Yale. The most extensively illustrated campuses are the University of Chicago (pages 1–11) and Princeton (pages 30–50). The scrapbook is preserved in the Duke University Archives and is invaluable for people interested in why Duke looks the way it does.

Representing the academicians, President Few and Professor Brown worked with Horace Trumbauer, architect, and the Olmsted Brothers, landscape architects, the professionals selected by James B. Duke.

Few people remember Horace Trumbauer today. But during the period between 1900 and 1930, his Philadelphia office received many prestigious commissions. Prior to beginning work at Duke, for example, he was responsible for residential designs for both William K. and Cornelius Vanderbilt, Perry Belmont, and P. A. B. Widener. He designed the Harry Elkins Widener Memorial Library at Harvard and the Philadelphia Museum of Art. Most significantly for the Duke commission were the residences he designed for James Buchanan Duke, a city home at Fifth Avenue and 78th Street in New York and plans for a large country estate in Somerville, New Jersey. Trumbauer's success with the establishment was extraordinary, for he had no academic training. He worked as a draftsman

West Campus elevations, Office of Horace Trumbauer

for G. W. and W. D. Hewitt of Philadelphia for six years before opening his own office in 1890. Like his more famous contemporaries, McKim, Mead & White, Trumbauer specialized in the manipulation of historical styles.

Why were different styles used on the two Duke campuses? In urban settings Trumbauer favored classically-based styles. His design for "Lynnewood Hall" (1898), in Elkins Park, Pennsylvania, for P. A. B. Widener was reputed to be the largest Georgian residence in America. But in rustic settings he often used the irregular silhouettes of the castellated Tudor or Gothic styles; Grey Towers (1894), in Glenside, Pennsylvania, inspired by Alnwick Castle in England, is a case in point. His preference for the rectilinear, classically-based styles when working among pre-existing streets and

West Campus, bird's-eye view, Office of Horace Trumbauer

East Campus bird's-eye view, Office of Horace Trumbauer

Scrapbook, University of Chicago Dining Hall, Professor Frank Clyde Brown

buildings may have been a factor in the decision to develop East Campus as a Georgian complex. On the other hand, the forested ridge designated as the site of the new West Campus made the Collegiate Gothic a natural choice. Stone, towers and finials, recesses and projections, deep shade and asymmetry—all were compatible with the wooded ridge.

Trumbauer's opinion, of course, was only part of the equation. President Few and Professor Brown were clearly impressed by the Collegiate Gothic buildings at both Princeton and the University of Chicago, and it may be worth noting that the Princeton campus was not far from James B. Duke's estate in New Jersey. (More information about design sources and Julian Abele, Trumbauer's principal designer, is included in Walks 1 and 3, following.)

Major decisions were made about the final layout of the two campuses at an on-site meeting, February 20–23, 1925. Here James B. Duke, Trumbauer, Brown, and Few were joined by Percival Gallagher, a landscape architect from the Olmsted Brothers; his record of the meeting re-creates the scene for us:

> Boarded Mr. Duke's private car at Newark 12–32 as arranged. . . . At West Philadelphia Mr. Trumbauer came aboard. Mr. Duke had with him Mr. Allen, his manager, or business associate, whom I had met in Mr. Duke's office, 511, Fifth Ave. on my first visit, when it was arranged I would make this preliminary visit to the ground for which the charge would be $150.00 per day, plus expenses. . . . We had excellent food on the car, and was told Mr. Duke had the best cook with him to be had anywhere.
>
> We all looked over a number of drawings Mr. Trumbauer brought, nearly all he had shown Mr. Duke before, for Trumbauer had been working on the problem for some months if not nearly a year. But they were all for the present Campus of Trinity College. This idea had but recently been abandoned and Trinity is to be made a Women's College in the Duke University and a wholly new site is to be built up as a Men's College. The purpose of the visit then was to determine this new site and to enable Mr. Duke to make decisions with respect to the options for land that Prof. Flower[s] had been taking on some 5000 odd acres of land southwest of Durham.
>
> The rebuilding of Trinity College will be in the Georgian Style, probably red brick, but the new college will be of stone and of the Collegiate Gothic Style in the scheme of which the church or chapel will occupy the central feature, with a notably tall tower of some architectural pretensions. At present we have nothing special to do at Trinity, but it may be that we will be asked to advise as to the grading. Trumbauer's scheme for this is pretty well determined by existing

West Campus, bird's-eye view, Office of Horace Trumbauer

buildings and other features. Mr. Duke's father, Mr. Washington Duke, was a benefactor of Trinity and in a central position on the main axis is a bronze statue of him sitting in a chair. . . . Dr. Brown, Professor of English at the College, who is giving a good deal of attention to the new college scheme and has immediate charge of the improvements to the grounds now going on the Trinity College Campus . . . has good ideas and has gathered a good deal of information bearing on the problem of the new college. In fact he and Professor Flower[s] had their eye quite definitely on the site finally determined upon, although no fixed ideas as to its utilization and approval. . . . The site for the buildings [on the new campus] was a wooded hill in the midst of a large area of open farmland, and was indeed an engaging proposition. . . . the summit area of the ridge . . . is to be the site.

Gallagher's report suggests that the decision to use two different styles was made before a final site was chosen for the West Campus and well before the Duke Endowment was official. This is not surprising, for President Few believed that surroundings affect character, and the potential influence of campus design was the subject of his graduation address to the class of 1931. He began that speech by observing that "some of the underlying ideas" that prompted the creation of the university "are illustrated in the buildings themselves." He stressed as well, "The builders of this University have sought to achieve physical beauty and unity and through these to suggest spiritual values. . . . The architectural harmony and strength of the plant is intended to suggest unity and fullness of life." Specifically, he noted that the compactness of the quadrangles "ought to make it natural for the students and teachers to think and work more and more from a common point of view rather than from the standpoint of conflicting interests." And speaking of the West Campus, he noted,

> The Chapel, hard by the library and the laboratories and cooperating with the University in its every effort to promote truth and serve humanity, is not only central, but, with its stained glass, its vaulted roof and noble spire, will dominate the place. This is intended to be symbolical of the truth that the spiritual is the central and dominant thing in the life of man.

West Campus

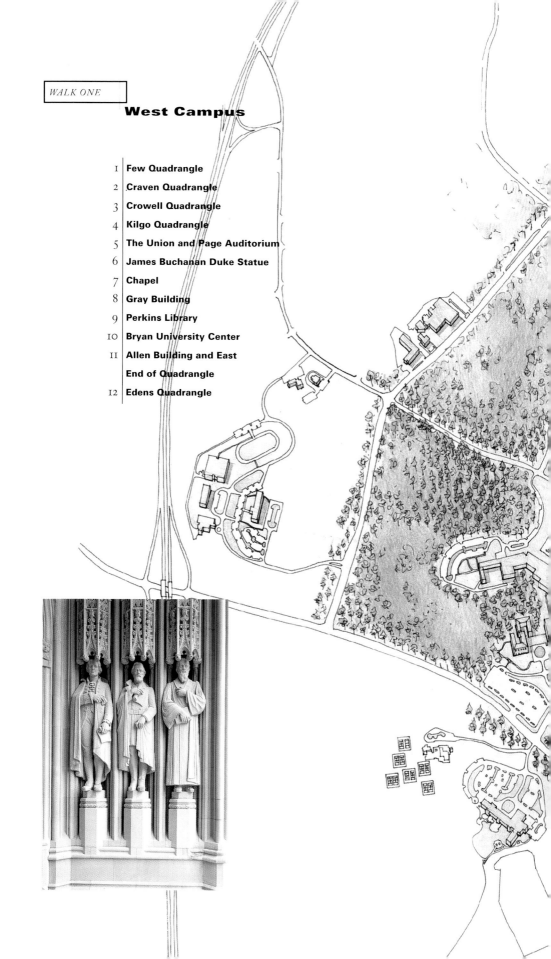

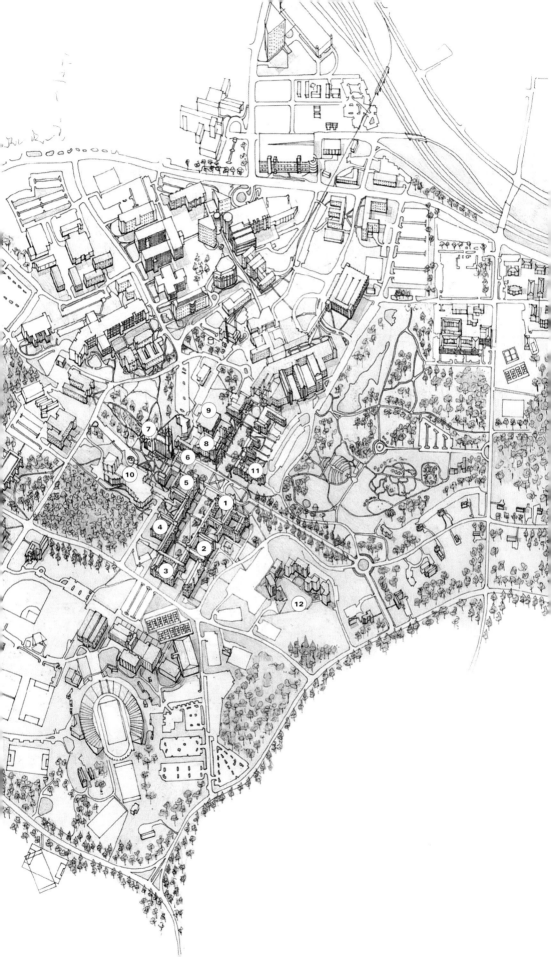

Plan, Style, and Architect

The word *campus* comes from the Latin word for a plane, a grassy country-side. Each area of the Duke campus is like a countryside unto itself—complex, yet internally coherent and comprehensible. A good way to get acquainted with how spaces and uses fit together and affect life is to imagine a bird's-eye overview and then focus in more closely on specific details.

West Campus was planned as two rectangular quadrangles laid across each other "in such a way that a person standing immediately in front of the Chapel can see the full length of all the quadrangles." The 1920s planning document that contains this guiding concept also notes that buildings defining the quadrangles should frame the top of the ridge, thereby taking advantage of the slopes to create basements without expensive excavations and to preserve "the very large, massive, virgin oaks on [top of] the plateau." The Chapel stands at the head of the cross-axis formed by the two main quadrangles. James B. Duke's 1924 directive is often quoted: "I want the central building to be a church, a great towering church which will dominate all the surrounding buildings." When you face the Chapel at the intersection of the quadrangles, the residential arm of the cross is on your left and the academic arm of the cross on your right. Generally speaking, this has been the pattern of use since West Campus opened in 1930.

The English Gothic style, the use of stone, towers, and archways all make West Campus architecturally a place apart. Why did they build it this way? Many other American institutions of higher learning—the Smithsonian Institution, Princeton University, Bryn Mawr, the University of Chicago—had or would use the Gothic style to suggest a kinship with the academic

Perkins Library, detail

traditions of medieval Oxford and Cambridge. President Few viewed the new Duke as an extension of these traditions. He wanted the campus to prompt people to think beyond local or regional roots; consequently, one finds signs of a broad intellectual heritage everywhere. Many buildings are ornamented with the shields, crests, or insignia of other institutions. The Gothic style is eminently suited to this use of emblematic ornament, for the style itself implies antiquity; it relies heavily on ornament; and moreover, its asymmetry, its nooks and crannies, create numerous focal points for the placement of memorial plaques and sculpture to serve as inspirational, visual epigrams of lives well lived.

The design of the buildings involved adaptation from numerous sources. Writing to Trumbauer's office, Frank Clyde Brown noted that the siting of West Campus made "the more rugged buildings at the University of Chicago" and "Warwick Castle [England] viewed from the South side" useful prototypes. To drive home his point, Brown mentioned showing these sources to James B. Duke, who "seemed very much pleased with all these pictures." With plans underway, Trumbauer sent a list of English buildings to George G. Allen, James B. Duke's assistant, who was in England at the time, and the architect said the list represented "the basis from which the designs of the men's university [West Campus] were inspired." In addition to Oxford and Cambridge, Trumbauer listed Eton College; Canterbury Cathedral and adjoining buildings; Wells Cathedral and Bishop's Close; Glastonbury Abbey near Wells; Lichfield Cathedral; Haddon Hall, Derbyshire; Much Wenlock Priory in Shropshire; Durham Cathedral; and the Chester Cathedral and Chester city walls and buildings. Trumbauer closed his letter to Allen by noting, "I would particularly like you to see the tower of Canterbury Cathedral as the tower of the chapel was suggested by the Canterbury spire."

Julian Francis Abele (1881–1950)

Who designed the original Gothic West Campus and the Georgian East Campus buildings? The contract for design and supervision was with Horace Trumbauer. As was customary at the time, the drawings are unsigned. Trumbauer's records have not survived, so there is no direct documentary evidence assigning credit to an individual or individuals in his office. Circumstantial evidence, however, suggests the chief design architect in Trumbauer's office, Julian F. Abele, was the principal creator.

Others who participated in the creation of the campus provide the most compelling evidence for attribution to Abele. In 1940, for example, when a question arose about the crypt in the Chapel, A. S. Brower, assistant to the comptroller, wrote that Abele should be contacted because he "prepared the plans for the building and . . . with his understanding of the building and all its details would be in a position to advise you better than anyone else." In the same vein, one of Trumbauer's assistants, Valentine B. Lee, Jr.,

Julian F. Abele

reminiscing to William E. King, "stated unequivocally that Julian Abele . . . designed the West Campus. Lee watched him sketch exterior detail on large drawings because one of Lee's jobs as a young draftsman was to take the finished exterior drawings when they were torn off a large roll of paper to the proper stations for the interior planning. He confirmed the fact that the business was run in the traditional manner of the time with everything going out under the name of the firm and only rarely credited to individuals."

Abele was born in Philadelphia and was in 1902 the first black graduate of the School of Architecture at the University of Pennsylvania. An outstanding student, he was president of the student Architectural Society and his drawings won numerous awards. When Abele finished at Penn, Trumbauer (who had no academic training himself) paid for him to study at the École des Beaux-Arts in Paris. Abele joined—or perhaps re-joined—Trumbauer's office in 1906 and was the chief design architect there from 1908 to 1938.

Although Duke administrators, like Brower, viewed Abele as responsible for buildings at Duke, he received little public recognition until 1988, and there is a poetic justice in the way his contribution came to light. Briefly, students protesting the Duke Endowment's investments in South Africa built prison-like shanties in front of the Chapel. Other students counter-protested, arguing the shanties defaced the campus and should be removed. The counter-protest prompted Susan Cook, a Duke undergraduate and Abele's great-grandniece, to write a letter to the *Duke Chronicle*. She noted that Abele had designed buildings at Duke and suggested he would not have objected to the shanties "because he was a victim of apartheid in this country. He was not so fortunate as you and I to travel freely across state borders. He never came to Duke to see what he had created because his revulsion of the segregated South made it impossible for him to travel further south than Philadelphia."

William E. King, Duke archivist, writes, "The following Spring Duke's Black Graduate and Professional Student Association initiated the annual Julian Abele Awards and Recognition Banquet, unveiling as part of the program, a commissioned portrait of Abele. President Brodie assisted in fundraising and agreed to the hanging of the portrait, the first of a black at Duke, in the foyer of Allen Building."

Stone and Stonework

When the time came to select building materials for Duke, small experimental walls were built to test a variety of stone for color and durability. The committee chose the slate-like, igneous stone from Hillsborough, North Carolina, about fifteen miles from Durham. It is dense and comes in some fourteen hues ranging from blue-gray to burnt sienna and ochre. The university's acquisition of the quarry ensured that it became a hallmark material for walls of all kinds at Duke, and it is still used extensively throughout the campus today. Cream-colored

Stonemasons at work on Chapel

Hillsborough stone

Indiana limestone was adopted for trim and framing elements. Soon an integral part of the institutional image, the early stonework set a high standard of design and construction that later Duke administrators and architects would wrestle with in a variety of ways.

Dyspeptic professors on the Union

John Donnelly, Sr., (1866–1947) of New York was the principal decorative stone contractor for West Campus. Before working at Duke, the Donnelly Company worked on the U.S. Supreme Court, the National Archives, the U.S. Post Office, and the Department of Justice in Washington, D.C., and the Federal Courthouse and Riverside Church in New York. John E. Donnelly, Jr., (1902–1970) apparently designed most of the architectural ornament at Duke, and his uncle, James Donnelly, served as an on-site supervisor.

Stonemasons, stonecutters, setters, and carvers had to be imported. The Hillsborough stone was roughly split and set by a team of approximately 100 masons, black and white, largely from North Carolina and West Virginia. The more exacting Indiana limestone was set by a smaller crew of ten to fifteen skilled Irish and Italian stone setters working for the Donnelly Company. Donnelly also employed five stone carvers to create the shields, gargoyles, and other ornament.

1. Few Quadrangle   *Office of Horace Trumbauer, 1938*

Going clockwise around the residential portion of the quadrangle, we appropriately begin with the set of buildings framing two interior court-yards or quads named in honor of William Preston Few (1867–1940). President of Trinity College from 1910 to1924 and of Duke University from

Few Quadrangle

1924 to 1940, he presented the idea of creating a research university to James B. Duke and subsequently worked with the trustees of the Duke Endowment to make the university a reality.

Like the rest of the main residential quadrangle, Few is in reality composed of a series of separate buildings sharing common walls. (There are some thirty-five residential buildings adjacent to the main quadrangle.) In the past, fraternities dominated this area. Now, however, there is a balanced population, male and female, independents and fraternities, sophomores to seniors. (All freshmen live on East Campus.)

Above the Few archways are figures carved in limestone—a pair of smiling students holding scrolls, an eagle, cross, and owl, for most of the original buildings on West Campus are enlivened by carved ornament.

2. Craven Quadrangle *Office of Horace Trumbauer, 1930*

An early Duke handbook of 1939 notes that Craven was called Fraternity Quad, as all but five of its sixteen houses served as headquarters for various fraternities. This area honors Braxton Craven (1822–1882), a determined educator and Methodist preacher, who transformed the Union Institute (a rural academy) into the Normal College in 1849 (with authority to grant state-approved teaching certificates) and then in 1859 into Trinity College, a liberal arts college affiliated with the Methodist Church. Often working in adverse circumstances, Braxton Craven created Trinity College, which, in turn, set the stage for the creation of Duke.

Craven Quadrangle, looking into Main Quadrangle

Main Quadrangle, looking into Few Quadrangle

Crowell Quadrangle

3. Crowell Quadrangle *Office of Horace Trumbauer, 1930*

When John F. Crowell (1857–1931), who was born in Pennsylvania and educated at Dartmouth and Yale, was chosen president of Trinity College in
1887, it was clear the trustees wanted Trinity to participate in educational
trends beyond the borders of rural Randolph County. Crowell introduced
and emphasized the then new social sciences, attracted an ambitious,
well-trained faculty, raised academic
standards, encouraged faculty
participation in public affairs, and,
seeking a more stimulating setting,
moved Trinity in 1890 to a new campus (on the site of today's East
Campus) with the support of Julian S.
Carr and Washington Duke. His tenure
as president lasted until 1894.

The Crowell quad exem-
plifies Trumbauer's formula for the
West Campus. The Crowell tower,
based on the St. Buryan Parish Church
in Cornwall, England, balances the
entrance tower of the medical school
at the far end of the main quadrangle.
Towers punctuate the quadrangles
and establish a rising and falling

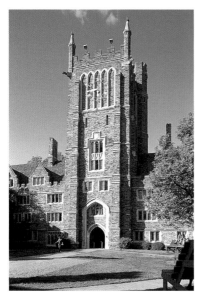

Crowell

silhouette, which effectively breaks the long facades into discrete parts. Crowell is a good spot to pause and appreciate the limestone ornament. Above the archway are six seals: medicine, law, religion, biology, the Duke family crest (three doves), and the Duke University seal (a cross, a rising sun, and a laurel wreath). And in the entrance arch and above Crowell's doorways are images of bearded professors teaching young men, as well as symbols of engineering, navigation or exploration, and nature.

4. Kilgo Quadrangle   *Office of Horace Trumbauer, 1930*

The names associated with the residential quads recount the history of Duke. When Crowell resigned as president of Trinity College in 1894, he was succeeded by John C. Kilgo (1861–1922), who served as president of Trinity from 1894 to 1910. Kilgo was a dynamic preacher and an energetic advocate of Christian education. During his administration, in 1896, Washington Duke gave Trinity an endowment of $100,000, with the stipulation that women be educated on an equal basis—as full-time, residential students. Washington Duke, who expressed unwavering support for Kilgo's administration, gave another $100,000 in 1898, and a similar amount in 1900. The growing endowment enabled the college to subsidize tuition and recruit students based increasingly on academic promise, attract a well-trained faculty, and erect new buildings on the present East Campus. (James B. Duke paid for the new Trinity Library—his first major contribution to the college.)

Kilgo Quadrangle

Kilgo Quadrangle, Collegiate Gothic roof details

Kilgo's courageous defense of academic freedom and his repudiation of racism during the "Bassett Affair" of 1903 remains inspiring today.

The exuberance of the ornament in Kilgo Quad seems appropriate, for his administration was anything but reticent. Here in stone we find one student studying, another playing a saxophone, Archimedes, athletes, an eagle and lion, the university shields of Emory, Clemson, William and Mary, and Tulane, as well as symbols of scholarship, justice, and assorted animals.

Corner of Modern Languages and Perkins Library

5. The Union and Page Auditorium

Office of Horace Trumbauer, 1930

All of the residence halls are secured twenty-four hours a day by a card-scanning lock system. The Union, however, is open and worth a visit, for here we can gauge changes in student lifestyles against the historic building style. The Union anchors the corner between the resident halls and the Chapel Court. The "General Conditions To Be Met" specified this sequence of uses—dormitories-Union-Chapel—and when the buildings were new, President Few said in 1931, "The University is built and organized with a compactness that ought to make it natural for the students and teachers to think and work more and more from a common point of view.... The Union is the social center for students and teachers alike."

Prior to the 1960s the student population was less mobile, less diverse, and more regimented than it is now. The stately oak-paneled dining halls in the Union evoke a time when three hot meals a day, served at set times, was the norm. Fraternities generally ate together, and the menu offered a limited range of traditional fare. Now, to satisfy radically changed eating habits, Duke's Auxiliary Services manages some twenty different food delivery sites (not including vending machines) with a wide array of menus. In addition to on-campus cafeterias and cafes, ten outside vendors participate in the university's flexible meal plan and make evening deliveries as late (or early) as 4AM.

Union at lunch time

Union exterior

Because at its inception everyone was expected to use the Union, it was an ideal place for meaningful ornament; consequently, here we find a veritable catalogue of shields, crests, and insignia. On the east elevation, from left to right are the university emblems of Geneva, Louvain, Oxford, Cambridge, Paris, Harvard, Yale, Princeton, Dartmouth College, and the University of Pennsylvania. On the north elevation, from left to right, are those of Virginia, North Carolina, Wofford, Furman, Randolph Macon, Wake Forest, Davidson, Vanderbilt, Washington and Lee, Emory, Henry, Sewannee, Texas, as well as the City of Durham and the State of North Carolina. On the west elevation, from left to right, can be found Guilford, Columbia, the Naval Academy, Cornell, Johns Hopkins, Chicago, Wisconsin, Michigan, and Stanford. Lastly, on the south elevation, from left to right, are Haverford and Millsaps. Shields of fourteen Cambridge University colleges are carved in the corbels of one dining hall, and sixteen college shields from Oxford are on the corbels of the other main dining hall.

Adjacent to the Union, the Page Auditorium boasted the best projection system in the southeast when the new campus opened. (The auditorium takes advantage of the slope of the ridge as suggested in the early planning documents.) College entertainment, however, like eating, is less communal today than it was in the 1930s (with the exception of sports events). During the 1970s the university began planning for a new university center (the Bryan Center) to accommodate small group and informal activities. The auditorium was named for Walter Hines Page, Trinity class of 1875, and his nephew Allison Page, Trinity class of 1920. Allison Page, killed in the battle of Belleau Wood, was the first Trinity undergraduate to die in World War I.

The statue is as simple and forthright as its inscription: "James Buchanan Duke, December 23, 1856–October 10, 1925. Industrialist, Philanthropist, Founder of the Duke Endowment."

Duke Statue

He is standing, relaxed, a cigar in his left hand (he smoked twenty-five a day) and a cane in his right, gazing toward the entrance of the university. The statue was created a decade after Duke's death by Charles Keck (1875–1951) who studied with Augustus Saint-Gaudens at the École des Beaux-Arts in Paris and at the Art Students' League in New York. Keck was a successful designer of aesthetically conservative, figural public monuments and memorial tablets.

The understated, laconic quality of the statue and inscription is apt, for James B. Duke avoided personal publicity. The pensive pose is also appropriate, for his achievements were based on keen insight and analysis, thorough planning, and meticulous execution.

The Duke Endowment represented the culmination of the Duke family's philanthropy, and it did more than create Duke University. Planning for the endowment began around 1915 and became official on December 11, 1924. Initially it consisted of a trust containing stock valued at approximately forty million dollars administered by fifteen trustees.

As guidance to the trustees, James B. Duke wrote:

> I have selected Duke University as one of the principal objects of this trust because I recognize that education, when conducted along sane and practical, as opposed to dogmatic and theoretical, lines, is, next to religion, the greatest civilizing influence. . . . And I advise that the courses at this institution be arranged, first, with special reference to the training of preachers, teachers, lawyers and physicians, because these are most in the public eye, and by precept and example can do most to uplift mankind, and second, to instruction in chemistry, economics and history, especially the lives of the great of earth, because I believe that such subjects will most help to develop our resources, increase our wisdom and promote human happiness.

James B. Duke stipulated other beneficiaries of the endowment including Davidson College, Furman University, Johnson C. Smith University, rural Methodist churches, pensions for retired Methodist ministers or their widows, and non-profit hospitals and orphanages for "both races" in North and South Carolina.

7. Chapel   *Office of Horace Trumbauer, 1932*

Begun in 1930, first used in 1932, and dedicated in 1935, the Chapel is one of the last great examples of the Collegiate Gothic style in America. Its design is a free adaptation of English Gothic with the 210-foot bell tower based on the Bell Harry Tower at Canterbury. Every day except Christmas the building is open to visitors. Monday through Friday the carillon (50 bells, 4 octaves) is played at 5PM. On Thursday at 5:15PM there is a choral vespers service. The Chapel is an active, functioning church. It hosts interdenominational worship services, conducted by religious leaders of all faiths, throughout the week. Chapel clergy also teach classes and lead worship services each Sunday.

In the Chapel at any time of day there are apt to be a handful of people sitting quietly, or peering at the gem-like windows, or moving unobtrusively from one detail to another. An attendant just inside the entrance answers questions, and several informative booklets are available.

The design of the Chapel is attributed to Julian Francis Abele (1881–1950), Trumbauer's chief designer. The first African American to attend the École des Beaux-Arts in Paris, Abele knew Gothic buildings firsthand. Many large, modern buildings lack the details that reward close

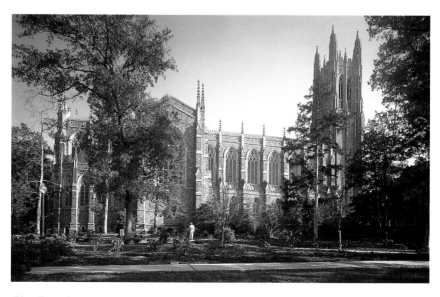

Chapel exterior

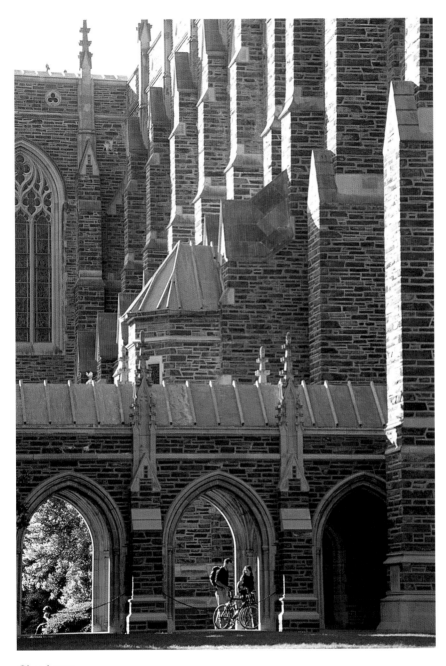

Chapel entry

scrutiny, but that is certainly not the case with the Chapel. John Donnelly was apparently responsible for designing the limestone figures framing the entry. He recalled that Trumbauer turned the matter over to him, and he sought advice from "a professor at Vanderbilt" (whose name Donnelly did not record). Above the entry from left to right are Thomas Coke (1747–1814), Francis Asbury (1745–1816), and George Whitefield (1714–1770), all of whom were instrumental in establishing the Methodist

Church in America. On the left side inside the porta, left to right, are the famous reformers Girolamo Savonarola (1452–1498) and Martin Luther (1483–1546), John Wycliffe (1324–1384), who translated the Bible, and directly above the door, John Wesley (1703–1791), founder of the Methodist Church. On the right hand side, inside the portal from left to right are Thomas Jefferson (1743–1826), Robert E. Lee (1807–1870), and the poet Sidney Lanier (1842–1881).

There is an interesting aside about Donnelly's carving of the figures. In 1988 a visitor noticed that the leftmost figure, which was supposed to represent Thomas Coke, Superintendent of the Methodist Mission in the United States, did not resemble his portraits. Looking into this observation, Duke researchers found that "Coke's" costume fit the mid-sixteenth-century judicial vestments appropriate to the period of Edward Coke, Lord Chief Justice of England (1552–1632). Why did Donnelly carve the wrong Coke? The answer is probably found on the bronze doors of the U.S. Supreme Court, where Donnelly created a relief on the right hand door, installed in 1935, entitled "Lord Coke and James I." Here Edward Coke is shown barring the King from the courtroom—a historic moment in the evolution of the separation of powers. Donnelly must have thought all Cokes were alike.

The Chapel interior is a full presentation of everything that makes the Gothic a highpoint of Western architecture. Its structural integrity is palpable. There is no structural steel in the walls or ceilings. The large open nave and aisles (291 feet long, sixty-three feet wide, and seventy-three feet high), with seating capacity for 1,470 people (and room for an additional 150 in the choir and fifty more in the Memorial Chapel), the expanse of stone, the vaulting height, and the subtly changing light all combine to create a place that resonates tranquility.

In the Gothic structural system, pointed arches, piers, columns, and buttresses carry most of the weight to the ground, making it possible to devote large areas within the walls to windows. Beautiful, symbol-laden stained glass is synonymous with Gothic religious buildings. G. Owen Bonawit of New York held the contract for the Chapel's seventy-seven stained glass windows, but personal papers in the Duke Archives indicate that one of his designers, S. Charles Jaekle, was the principle creator. The uppermost or clerestory windows present Old Testament subjects; the

Chapel nave and aisles

Memorial Chapel

windows in the aisles are devoted to the New Testament; the large transept and chancel windows contain figures from both the Old and New Testaments; and the narthex windows depict scenes from the life of Jesus, and others portray women from the Old Testament. Taken all together, the windows contain more than 800 figures and over one million pieces of glass. It took fifteen craftsmen almost three years to make and install the windows.

The Memorial Chapel is located at the south end of the nave (the far end, left-hand corner from the main entrance). Here marble effigies of Washington Duke and his sons Benjamin Newton Duke and James

The Chapel's carillon being installed

Buchanan Duke lie on top of their sarcophagi. The Memorial Chapel was added to the plans after the death of James Duke, and friends and admirers contributed funds for its construction. Charles Keck carved the three tombs from Carrara marble. Samuel Yellin (1885–1945), one of America's greatest blacksmiths, made the wrought-iron grille separating the Memorial Chapel from the nave. The choir stalls and decorative carving in lime and oak was designed by Charles H. Crowther and made by Irving and Casson–A.H. Davenport, Inc.

A crypt, open to the public, is located beneath the Memorial Chapel. Here William Preston Few, the first president, J. Deryl Hart, the fourth president, Terry Sanford, the sixth president of Duke, Governor of North Carolina, and U. S. Senator, and Mrs. Nanaline Holt Duke, the widow of James Buchanan Duke, are buried, and the ashes of other university notables are interred. A handrail carved into the stone wall of the crypt stairway literally puts the visitor in touch with the quality of the construction of the Chapel.

The Duke Chapel organs and carillon are widely known. There are three principal organs, each representing a specific structural type designed for different musical styles and settings. The original Aeolian organ of 1932 has some 7,000 pipes on either side of the chancel. It is designed for full-bodied, post-Romantic music. The Flentrop organ of 1976, located in the arch between the narthex and the nave, has 5,000 pipes. In construction and tone it resembles an eighteenth-century Dutch or French instrument. The

Carillon

Brombaugh organ of 1997 has 960 pipes; it is an Italian Renaissance-style instrument. Located in the Memorial Chapel, the Brombaugh organ is designed for intimate presentations.

Pealing bells marking the end of the working day represent the sound of Duke for many people. Duke's carillon consists of fifty bells and was one of the earliest concert-sized instruments to be installed in the United States. Although the art form is centuries old in Belgium and Holland, it has only experienced popularity in the United States during the twentieth century. The English bell foundry John Taylor and Company, one of the largest and oldest bell foundries in the world, cast Duke's bells. The largest weighs over 11,000 pounds and the smallest only ten pounds. The carillonneur plays the bells, which hang stationary in the tower, from a keyboard or clavier—depressing a key pulls a wire, which pulls the hammer, or clapper, against the side of the bell. Duke has enjoyed two excellent carillonneurs over its history. Anton Brees, a master carillonneur from Belgium, inaugurated the instrument and continued to play for special occasions until his death in 1965. Since then J. Samuel Hammond, the Rare Book Librarian at Duke, has continued the tradition. Hammond began playing the carillon as an undergraduate in the 1960s and became the official university carillonneur in 1986.

8. Gray Building

Office of Horace Trumbauer, 1930;
Six Associates, addition, 1964–1972

The clear definition of space created by quadrangles is satisfying, but it also makes changes or additions difficult. Seeking more space, most West Campus academic units have moved from their original quarters. The department of religion and the School of Divinity, however, have both remained next to the Chapel, and the Divinity School has successfully expanded to the rear. In 1964 the interiors of the contiguous buildings were renovated, the mechanical systems were upgraded, and the architects, Six Associates of Asheville,

Gray Building

Gray addition

added a projecting, limestone-faced Gothic porch to make the entrance
defining the Divinity School more prominent. The Divinity School entrance
is thus the only element of the West Campus quadrangles not designed by
the Trumbauer firm.

Six Associates also designed the 35,000-square-foot addition to the
rear of the Divinity School. This new wing—really a new building doubling
the facilities—was completed in 1972. The new wing is best viewed from
the parking lot behind the building, where it can be compared to the Perkins
Library addition. By 1970 dissatisfaction was mounting with the use of pre-
fabricated panels of Hillsborough stone; announcements for the Divinity
School addition were careful to note that it was "to be finished in laid-up
rather than pre-fabricated Hillsborough stone slabs . . . similar in exterior
appearance to nearby existing structures—both old and new—including the
Duke Chapel, Perkins Library, and the Divinity School's new library adjoining Perkins and old Gray Building."

As noted earlier, James B. Duke indicated that the training of
ministers formed an essential part of his vision for the university. Today
the Divinity School enrolls some 500 students in four graduate programs.
Its library is well known for its collections in patristics, Quakerism, Egypt-
ian archaeology, Buddhism, Judaic studies, ancient Greek manuscripts,
and Wesleyiana.

The Gray section of the building is named in honor of James
Alexander Gray, Sr., a member of the three-person committee of man-
agement that sustained Trinity College in the late nineteenth century. He
was a founder and president of Wachovia National Bank and an active
Methodist layman.

Perkins Library

9. Perkins Library

Office of Horace Trumbauer, 1930; addition, 1948; Perry, Shaw, Hepburn & Stewart, with Caudill, Rowlett and Scott, addition, 1969

Perkins Library, the central library in the Duke University system, is strategically located opposite the Union, between the residential and academic arms of the ridge-top quadrangle. Its main entrance stood originally in the base of the tower where the Chapel courtyard joins the academic arm of the quadrangle. Above this entry are figures holding a globe and a book.

The library has been added onto twice. In 1948 a $1.5 million gift from Mary Duke Biddle funded an expansion behind the original library, which increased the capacity to 850,000 volumes. In 1969 a six-story, 200,000-square-foot new building costing $8.7 million was built behind and connected to the existing library. Perry, Shaw, Hepburn & Stewart of Boston designed this 1969 addition, with Caudill, Rowlett and Scott as associate architects. Using the slope of the land, they effectively screened the new

Perkins Library Gothic Reading Room

building in the angle behind Gray, Perkins, and the old Law School (the addition is visible in the gap to the left between the old Law and Chemistry buildings as you approach Davison).

The current main entrance lies through an exhibition lobby-corridor that ties the old and new units together. The entrance leads to the circulation and reference departments, on-line catalogues, reading areas, and a bank of elevators that give access to stack and administrative levels in both the old and new sections. The building includes more than a dozen rooms set aside as study rooms for departments in the humanities and social sciences, seminar and word-processing rooms, several audio-visual classrooms, the University Archives, and the Rare Book, Manuscript, and Special Collections Library. Perkins is consistently ranked among the top twenty research libraries in the country; it can accommodate 2,100 readers and Duke collections exceed 2.5 million volumes.

Just as trees have unseen roots mirroring the spread of branches above ground, the out-of-sight resources of libraries support and sustain universities. On West Campus four branch libraries focus on the sciences: the Biological and Environmental Sciences Library (botany, zoology, ecology, molecular and cell biology, environmental sciences, forestry, hydrology, and meteorology), the Chemistry Library, the Vesic Engineering Library (including both computer science and engineering), and the Mathematics and Physics Library (including astronomy, astrophysics, and statistics). Another science branch, the Pearse Memorial Library, is located in Beaufort, North

Carolina. At the Duke Marine Laboratory, its collections include marine biology, marine biotechnology, oceanography, botany, biochemistry, oceanography, and marine botany and biochemistry. Professional school libraries on or adjacent to West Campus include the Divinity School Library in the Gray Building, the Fuqua School of Business Library, the School of Law Library, and the Medical Center Library. On East Campus there are two libraries, the Lilly Library (for art history, film, theater, and philosophy) and the Music Library (including musical scores and the Music Media Center).

Altogether the Duke library system contains more than 4.7 million volumes and has an annual materials budget of more than nine million dollars. Researchers are not restricted to these collections, however, for internet connections are available throughout the library system and everyone with a Duke card has access to the Triangle Research Library Network, connecting them to the holdings of the University of North Carolina at Chapel Hill, North Carolina State University, and North Carolina Central University.

To get a sense of Perkins, visitors may want to pause and look at the displays in the entrance lobby, then visit the on-line catalog and reference area just inside the entry. Going back through the entrance lobby, take the hallway to the right to see the Rare Book Room on the ground floor and climb the tower stairs—the original entry—to the Gothic Reading Room on the second floor. Pause and sit in the Gothic Reading Room; lofty and book-lined, it is as tranquil and silent as an aquarium. Just outside the Gothic Reading Room, as if in conscious contrast, is the Perk, a corridor adapted as a lounge and popular coffee shop.

The Perk

In a setting as harmonious and revered as West Campus, the university is continually challenged to accommodate expansion and changing uses. The Perkins addition provides a cameo portrait of this problem and one response to it.

When expansion became necessary in the late 1940s few Americans were talking about "architectural context" or "a sense of place." The university's new construction at mid century—the functional brick boxes of Engineering (1948), Physics (1949), Biological Sciences (1962), and Law (1963)—reflected a belief that physical separation from the historic quadrangles, a green-belt buffer, and the cost of stone and ornament all justified a break with tradition. The community reacted unfavorably, however. The *Duke Chronicle* remarked that the new buildings "subtracted severely from the effect of the original theme." Consequently, the trustees commissioned a master plan in 1963 to recommend design criteria as a guide for future construction. The analysis and recommendations by Caudill, Rowlett and Scott of Houston have influenced almost everything subsequently built near West Campus.

The Caudill report identified a "vocabulary of forms" or visual characteristics which make the historic West Campus appealing. They noted that these characteristics should "serve as a stimulus"—not a strait-jacket—to make new designs compatible with the historic buildings. Their report discussed:

> Vertical Emphasis (towers, projecting bays, buttress, pinnacles and chimneys, vertically shaped doors and windows)

> Human Scale ("The individual scale of the older buildings is faithful to the Gothic, which was based on the size of a man's hand. This is one of

Perkins Library addition

the roots of its appeal and the reason that even the loftiest cathedral still retain[s] a sense of human scale." Or again, "The over-all scale of the campus will depend ultimately on whether the university plan will be based on a pedestrian scale or an automobile scale.")

Richness (ornament, juxtaposition of different materials, and the use of projection and recession to create defining lines or shapes of shadow and shade)

Variety (stone of many hues and sizes, differently shaped windows, doorways, asymmetrical plans and silhouettes)

Unity (the conscious variation of a limited set of materials and forms to create a fugue-like pattern)

They also emphasized, "A campus is composed of exterior rooms as well as interior rooms" and "the Gothic Campus illustrates this point vividly . . . [with its] good spaces, approaches and vistas."

They followed their analysis of each characteristic of West Campus Gothic by recommendations as to how a similar effect could be obtained using contemporary materials and techniques. Reflective of the period in which they wrote, their interest lay in the psychology of style rather than in the historical associations that captivated President Few and his peers.

10. Joseph M. and Kathleen Price Bryan University Center

Hayes–Howell and Associates, 1990

Sustaining growth and change within a historic setting is an on-going challenge for Duke. With this in mind, it is instructive to visit the university union, the Bryan Center, while the additions to Perkins and the Divinity School are fresh in the mind's eye.

In 1952 when the central administration moved into the then new Allen Building, offices in Flowers were remodeled to expand the Page Auditorium and union complex, but this solution proved short-lived. The expanding student body quickly outgrew the space originally allotted to student activities. By 1970 a student and faculty committee was planning a wholly new, up-to-date facility.

The criteria developed for the Bryan Center reflected an analysis of information concerning eighty new student unions across the country. Members of the committee visited the sixteen unions that appeared to be the most successful. They concluded that the new union needed to be accessible from the quadrangle, be located as near the center of campus

Bryan University Center, reference and current periodicals, top, *student lounge and outdoors patio,* bottom

as possible, and be designed to minimize its impact on the landscape. The new union also needed to accommodate an array of activities, including theaters, shops, a rathskeller, a gallery, places to sit, read, and talk, lecture and banquet halls, a post office, and meeting rooms.

In 1972, sixteen architectural firms competed for the project. The university selected Hayes-Howell and Associates of Southern Pines as principal architects in association with Caudill, Rowlett and Scott (CRS), the Houston firm that authored the design study on making new construction compatible with the historic setting. After a protracted period of fund raising, the new union was dedicated in 1982.

Stone panel

The Bryan Center is screened from the quadrangles much like the additions to the Divinity School and Perkins Library. But the new union is different inasmuch as it is not contiguous to its on-the-quadrangle counterpart. Instead, one accesses the Bryan Center via an elevated, umbilical cord-like walkway, which emphasizes the discordant horizontally of its exterior. It is difficult to understand how CRS reconciled this windowless, rectilinear principal elevation with its design analysis and recommendations for Duke.

The interior, which has been remodeled several times, achieves the goals of the student-faculty planning committee. The committee had sought "the feeling ... of coming into a busy street scene." Upon entering, visitors are drawn inward toward the light, for most of the wall opposite the entry is glass and looks into the trees. A variety of choices immediately confronts the visitor. Tiered balconies present a dramatic perspective down over the rathskeller, onto the outdoor patio, and into woods beyond.

Bryan interior

11. Allen Building and east end of Quadrangle

Quadrangle *Office of Horace Trumbauer, 1930*
Allen Building *Office of Horace Trumbauer, 1954*

Davison comprises the east end of the main quadrangle. As the original entrance to the medical facilities, it is discussed at the beginning of the Medical Center Walk.

Next to Perkins is the Language Building (originally the Law School) and the old Chemistry Building. Opposite Perkins is Allen, which houses the central administration, the Graduate School offices, Classical Studies, and much of the English department. Adjacent to Allen are the Social Sciences Building and the Sociology/Psychology Building. The academic buildings, extending the Gothic pattern of the whole, do not call attention to themselves.

The completion of the Allen Building in 1954 marked the erection of the final building on the quadrangle. Architecturally, it is a seamless extension of the original plans—an unsurprising fact, for it is said to be the last building designed by Julian Abele, who died in 1950. The building is named in honor of George G. Allen (1874–1960), first chairman of the Duke Endowment, personal counselor to James B. Duke, president of the Duke Power Company, and a Duke University trustee for thirty-two years.

12. Edens Quadrangle

Edens Quadrangle *Six Associates, 1966*
Schaeffer Dormitory *John Rogers Associates, 1989*

A cluster of seven dormitories, Edens Quadrangle was one of the first attempts to adapt the CRS recommendations to modern construction. The use of Hillsborough stone and cast concrete in this quadrangle would be repeated with variations for the next thirty years. Edens was designed to house approximately 400 students in suites—bedrooms grouped around a sitting room and balcony. Two of the dormitories have become "affinity dorms," with Mitchel residents focusing on the arts and Decker residents

Edens Quadrangle and Schaeffer Dorm

Edens Quadrangle

emphasizing foreign languages. The topographical features that make Edens picturesque—the buildings are sited astride a stream in a dell—also make them feel a bit "cut off" from West Campus proper.

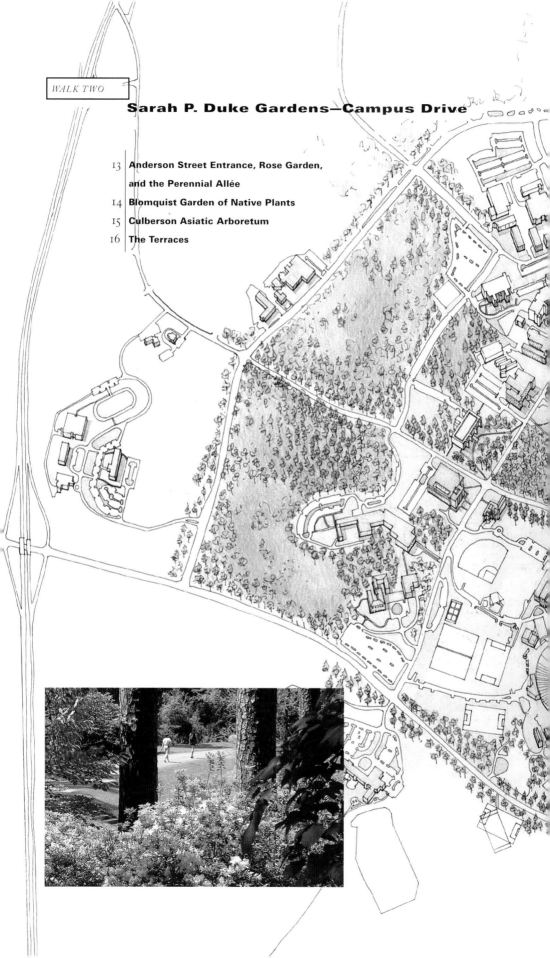

Sarah P. Duke Gardens—Campus Drive

Campus Drive

The Sarah P. Duke Gardens should be on every visitor's list of things to see at Duke. The main entrance is located on Anderson Street, near the corner of Anderson and Campus Drive. Parking is available just inside the entrance. Alternative nearby parking can be found at the Medical Complex Parking Deck on Trent Drive, and, on weekends, at the open parking lots on Campus and Flowers Drives. Gates provide pedestrian access from Lewis Street (the residential Central Campus) and from Flowers Drive (West Campus and the Medical Complex). The garden is open every day, 8AM to dusk, year-round, free of charge. The Durham Chamber of Commerce estimates that approximately 300,000 people visit the Gardens each year. Most visitors simply amble through, but both public and private tours are available, and provisions have been made for handicap access. For details call 919.684.3698; general recorded information is available any time; operators answer specific questions during office hours, 8AM–4:30PM, Monday–Friday.

The Gardens cover approximately fifty-five acres of rolling land in the dell below the east slope of the West Campus ridge. The original Trumbauer-Olmsted Brothers plans for the West Campus show Chapel Drive—the main entrance—accented by dramatic water features such as fountains, spillways, and ponds—all of which were omitted to save money. Strictly speaking, the present Gardens are not an outgrowth of the original plans; nonetheless, the Gardens share with the Trumbauer-Olmsted plans an adaptation of the terrain to create a botanical and topographical counter-point to the architectural setting of West Campus.

When West Campus opened, the site of the Gardens was undeveloped woodlands. Frederic M. Hanes, a neurologist and chairman of the department of medicine, was the first to promote the creation of a garden in the southern end of the ravine, where the original plans had shown a lake. Hanes lived in the house now used by Alumni Affairs (and later in the house occupied by the Development office). Going to and from the hospital and medical school every day, he became intimately familiar with the site. Interested in irises, he arranged for John C. Wister, president of the American Iris Society, to visit and make recommendations. It is worth noting that Duke botanist Hugo L. Blomquist objected to a garden devoted solely to irises, arguing that a meaningful garden should be professionally planned, feature a variety of plants, and not be "the object of one person's hobby."

The Great Depression made it difficult to get the project underway, especially because, as Wister noted, the site was prominent, and whatever was done had to be well-executed and maintained. Hanes persisted. He obtained a $20,000 gift from Sarah P. Duke, the widow of Benjamin Duke, and her interest prompted the trustees of the Duke Endowment and the university to approve the project and provide the remainder of the funding. Work began in 1934, and under the direction of Norfleet Webb 40,000 irises,

Ellen B. Shipman, landscape architect

25,000 daffodils, and 10,000 additional bulbs and annuals were planted in what is now the South Lawn.

This first phase of the Gardens was short-lived, for flooding and disease quickly convinced Hanes that bulbs would not flourish here. Sarah P. Duke died in 1936, and working with her daughter, Mrs. Mary Duke Biddle, Hanes retained Ellen B. Shipman to design a more formal and substantial garden honoring Sarah P. Duke on higher ground north of the ill-fated first plantings. The Terraces, designed by Shipman, opened in 1939. This feature, the oldest part of the Gardens, is for many visitors the highlight.

Ellen B. Shipman was among the first generation of women landscape architects in America. Her practice was based in Philadelphia and Cornish, New Hampshire. At Duke, using Hillsborough stone, she created terraces stepping down the hillside from a pergola; she designed the flanking service buildings, the pond at the foot of the terraces, and she conceived (and retained Frederic P. Leubuscher to design and install) a rock garden facing the terraces across the pond. The formal, symmetrical design of the Terraces draws on Italian Renaissance models. The asymmetrical pool and rock garden, however, was inspired by a more informal tradition, perhaps the English eighteenth-century Picturesque or Chinese or Japanese gardens. The juxtaposition of diverse garden types has continued as the Gardens have developed; consequently, today they are like a quilt composed of interlocking areas, each offering something unique to the pattern of the whole.

13. Anderson Street Entrance, Rose Garden, and the Perennial Allée

William B.S. Leong, 1959; Edith Eddleman and Douglas Ruhren, 1999

Just to the left of the main entrance is a polished granite bench dedicated to Professor Paul Kramer, whose tenure as director coincided with the expansion of both the goals and extent of the Gardens. He was a plant physiologist and when appointed director by the trustees in 1945 it was with the understanding that he would make the Gardens useful as well as ornamental. Kramer initiated a program of labeling, public outreach, and presentation of the native flora. Working with a staff of horticulturists, he began to develop paths and plantings into the woods adjacent to the site occupied by Shipman's terraces and pond.

The expanded program was well received, and in 1959 the trustees officially allocated a total of fifty-five acres to the Gardens. That year William

Perennial Allée

B. S. Leong of Boston prepared a master plan for the expanded Gardens. He opened the Anderson Street access, and by doing so provided a distinctly public entrance with a vista of the Chapel tower. Here the gates of Hillsborough stone and ironwork incorporating Gothic arches evoke the West Campus and open upon a broad path flanked by linden trees and perennial beds designed by Edith Eddleman and Douglas Ruhren. Conceived as longitudinal gardens in themselves, these beds contain over 1,400 plants, offer something of interest at every season, and constitute a gallery of species potentially useful to the home gardener. The Perennial Allée leads down a slight incline to a circular rose garden, a hub from which visitors can branch out in several directions. The Gardens contain some five miles of pathways, so visitors may want to select objectives and follow the map.

14. Blomquist Garden of Native Plants   *1968*

Just south of the Rose Garden is the H. L. Blomquist Garden of Native Plants. The Leong master plan showed this as an area devoted to ferns and native trees. In 1968, friends and former students of Duke's first botanist, Hugo Leander Blomquist (1885–1964), began developing an area now covering six-and-a-half acres, devoted to native plants, in his honor. The Blomquist Garden today contains 910 kinds of plants native to the southeastern United States and has its own curator, Edwin F. Steffek. His

Blomquist Garden gazebo

Blomquist Garden of Native Plants, entry

paperback checklist provides a thorough catalogue of the collection. At
the heart of this section of the
Gardens, a pavilion beside a small
pond with millstone stepping stones
is well worth a side trip. The pavilion
was designed by Linda Jewell, professor of landscape architecture at
University of California, Berkeley; the
pond was made by Edwin Steffek;
and the millstones were donated by
the family of Wiliam Leong. Another
special spot in the Blomquist Garden
is a bird-watching pavilion. This
playful open structure, perched above
a ravine, resembles a birdhouse on

Bird-watching pavilion

a human scale. It was designed by Sam Reynolds, landscape architect, and donated by the Irving E. Alexander family in memory of Pearl Fisher Alexander.

The Blomquist Garden is an enchanting place characterized by dappled sunlight filtering through the trees, small ponds, ferns, and aquatic plants.

15. Culberson Asiatic Arboretum

William Louis Culberson, 1978–1995

Asiatic Arboretum

In 1978 William Louis Culberson, a Duke botanist, succeeded Paul Kramer as director of the Gardens. The present northern end of the Gardens, the ponds, dam, and Asiatic Arboretum are visible fruits of Culberson's inspiration, dedication and executive ability during his tenure, which ran from 1978 to 1995.

By creating the dam, Garden, and north ponds, Culberson simultaneously solved the problem of flooding (which had grown worse over the years as more and more land was paved near the Gardens) and introduced large-scale water features—the glistening reflection of which all cultures appear to find satisfying at an elemental level. Culberson carefully planted these approximately twenty acres to suggest relationships between many species of Asiatic and American plants, a subject which has long fascinated botanists. Here some 550 species of Asiatic plants may be seen in a setting accented by lanterns, teahouses, and bridges, which evoke a Japanese tea garden. Especially notable are the Ayamebashi, or Iris Bridge, the Koyabo Lantern (a small hut stone lantern), and stone work along the garden stream. Linda Jewell designed the master plan for the Asiatic Arboretum's pathways. Paul Jones, horticulturalist in charge of this area, designed and installed the streamside Hillsborough stone outcroppings so artfully that they appear antediluvian, naturally weathered in place.

The Terraces

16. The Terraces   *Ellen B. Shipman, 1939*

Ellen Shipman's terraces remain the most architectonic and dramatic feature in the Gardens. Here the impact is based upon the extensive use of
stone, contrasting plant materials (spire-like conifers and colorful, horizontally disposed bedding plants), water, and a notable change in elevation.
Shipman's principal entrance through the wisteria-covered pergola is still
splendid, with its broad flight of steps descending to the pool. But perhaps
a distant view, revealing the structure of the whole, is most memorable.
Robert F. Durden, Duke historian and author of a brief history of the

Pergola

Gardens, captures the drama of "terraces spilling downward with flowers. Each terrace ... a horizontal band of stone accented by broad stripes of color. Seasonal plantings keep a continuity of color throughout the year, and while the spring show of tulips and pansies is always splendid, nothing quite rivals the terraces filled with richly-colored chrysanthemums in the autumn. When seen from the western hilltop, in the late afternoon's golden sunlight, the terraces then become a breathtaking sight, a multicolored tapestry surrounded by elegant magnolia trees and soaring pines."

At the foot of the Terraces, north of the pond, stands the half-century-old Dawn Redwood (*Metasequoia glyptostroboides*). Its bulging, serpentine roots and limbs evoke images of constrained energy like a statue by Michelangelo. It is a memorable tree. The tree was thought to have become extinct several million years ago, but in the 1940s a Chinese forester discovered a single specimen in a temple in a remote Szechuan village; an American government expedition secured seeds for its propagation in the United States.

Dawn Redwood

President Few's house, now Undergraduate Admissions

Campus Drive and Central Campus Housing

Most visitors will see Campus Drive and Central Campus Housing from their cars or the bus as they come and go between East Campus and West Campus. The university developed Campus Drive to connect the two campuses, and built nine houses along it—and two more along Chapel Drive—for faculty and administrators. The Trumbauer firm designed the house now used by Undergraduate Admissions (2138 Campus Drive), as a president's residence. William Preston Few first occupied it. Across the street at 2127 Campus Drive, the Trumbauer office also designed the house originally for the treasurer (and later president) Dr. Robert Lee Flowers, now occupied by the university's Development Office. At the corner of Chapel Drive and University Road, 614 Chapel Drive, the architects designed the house for Dr. Frederic M. Hanes, first head of the department of medicine, which is currently the Alumni Office. Trumbauer's office also designed the residence at the northwest corner of Campus Drive and Anderson Street, presented used as the International House.

Today Campus Drive exemplifies adaptive use, a key strategy in historic preservation. The former

Collegiate Gothic gables and rooflines

 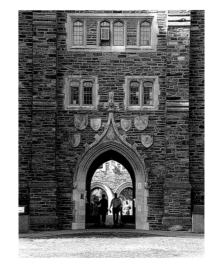

Crowell Quadrangle, two entrances

residence along Campus Drive now serve other uses, but the streetscape's quiet, residential character has been preserved as a beneficial border for the south side of West Campus.

Most of the 540 apartments that make up Central Campus Housing are located between Alexander and Oregon Streets along Erwin Road, an area formerly occupied by Erwin Mill workers' housing. The complex was completed in 1972, and was designed to accommodate married students with children, so parking is largely located on the perimeter and the interior is planted and landscaped with playgrounds. Although architecturally undistinguished—resembling low-rise townhouse apartments in Anywhere USA—the buildings make good use of sight screens to maximize privacy.

East Campus

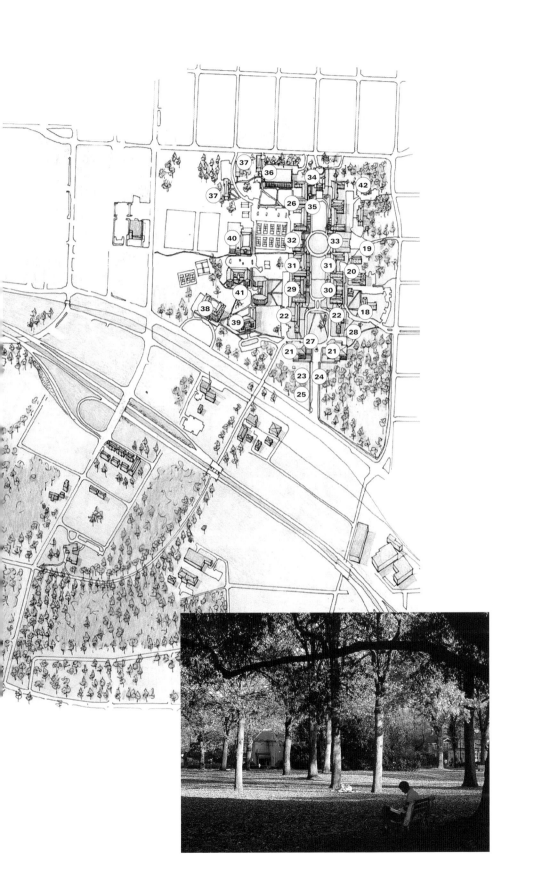

Campus bus loading on East Campus

Duke University Transit System

Throughout the day, with each change of class, buses and vans operated by the Duke University Transit System transport approximately 2,000 students between the East and West campuses. The system is free for students, staff, and visitors, and buses run on scheduled five- to fifteen minute intervals (depending on route and time of day) from 7:15AM until 2AM. After hours, free van shuttle service is available upon request. The twenty-two buses log more than 40,000 miles per year, since the network of routes covers Central Campus, outlying parking areas, the Medical Center and Science Drive, as well as East and West campuses, and the buses may be chartered by student organizations. Master schedules are available at the Bryan Center.

Vestiges of Trinity College

Architecturally speaking, the university began on the eastern fringes of East Campus. Duke—like America—moved (and is still moving) westward. Epworth (1892), Crowell (1892), and the Ark (1898) formed part of the core of Trinity College, but the 1925 Trumbauer plan turned its back on them, and they have lain off the beaten track for seventy-five years. Undisturbed, they have been allowed to slide into a state of genteel decrepitude.

Today these three buildings provide a benchmark for gauging the architectural aspiration of the new university. Visitors who enjoy a sense of context may want to begin their tour of the East Campus here.

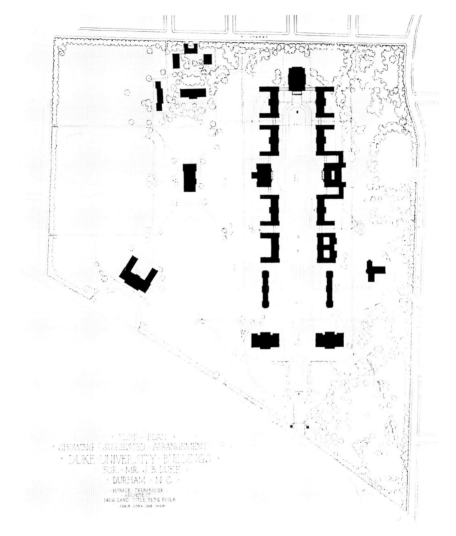

East Campus plan, 1925

Epworth stands much diminished, and its facade has been simpli-fied by the application of stucco. But Crowell, which resembles a small, brick turn-of-the-century mill, and the Ark, a wooden frame and clapboard build-ing, are both intact. It is obvious that the original buildings were not coordi-nated by site plan, style, or materials. Furthermore, they were all vernacular in scale and craftsmanship. This *ad hoc*, informal, local character of the older Trinity buildings was rejected when the time came to create a complex uni-versity organized along national and international lines. The creators of Duke were influenced by universities emphasizing graduate education and research in addition to undergraduate instruction, and the layout of new campus plans can be likened to a complex organizational chart with straight lines linking boxes in a well thought-out pattern.

Trinity College had experienced a burst of growth just before World War I. The East and West Campus buildings and Jarvis and Aycock residence halls, all designed by North Carolina architect C. C. Hook, bear witness to this last florescence of Trinity. But Hook's four buildings, like the nineteenth-century Trinity facilities, did not fit the image the creative Washington Duke had in mind.

The Georgian Style

The creators left no explanation as to why they chose the Georgian style for the campus developed beyond Jarvis and Aycock. Several things must have come into play. First, like a proscenium arch, the East and West Duke buildings created a classically inspired frame for the site; secondly, many people identified the Georgian style with the colonial era, the founding fathers, and revered national and local institutions; and finally, the level site and nearby rectilinear grid of streets and lots must have made the Georgian style seem harmonious. In any event, the Trumbauer firm used the sight lines created by C. C. Hook's four grouped buildings to develop the East Campus mall.

Like Jefferson's design for the University of Virginia, East Campus mall has a rotunda—the Baldwin Auditorium—closing its long, open rectangle. Both long sides of the rectangle are composed of five buildings, each a mirror image of its opposite across the lawn. These eleven buildings are all built of red brick with white, Vermont marble trim, and slate roofs. Entering the East Campus from Main Street, between the East and West Duke buildings, beyond Aycock and Jarvis, you first encounter a matched pair of academic buildings, then a pair of dormitories on either side of the mall, then

East Campus mall

the matching library (on the left), and Union (on the right), then more matched dormitories, and finally the Auditorium closing the vista. East Campus was planned as a women's college, and that is how it was used from 1930 to 1972. With dormitories, classrooms, library, Union, and an auditorium, it provided everything needed by students in residence. In the educational terminology of the time, this was a "co-ordinate" women's college, separate and presumed equal—like Radcliffe College at Harvard University or Barnard at Columbia.

The mall exemplifies the visual and conceptual clarity of the Georgian Style. Its buildings are almost symmetrical in plan and elevation. Their marble ornament stands out crisply against the brick and defines patterns that are repeated from building to building. Everything within the mall is open to view, linear, and well defined, and the resulting impression is one of order and repose, control and balance.

Today the East and West campuses create quite different impressions, but the difference is not simply a matter of style. Although West Campus cost approximately four times more to build than East Campus ($16.4 million for West Campus and $4.8 million for East Campus), there is nothing in the historical records to suggest the creators intended to make West Campus a nicer place to live and work. It is true, however, that all anecdotes about James B. Duke's participation—leading men through bushes and leaping ditches—focus on the West Campus site. Breaking the new ground must have been exciting, and the creators no doubt found the rolling topography and undeveloped woodlands more dramatic than the level fairgrounds behind Trinity.

To the advantages of setting and the drama of the Gothic style, West Campus added the central institutional functions—the administration, the main library, the larger Union, the basketball gym and football stadium—and the most memorable focal points—the Chapel and the Sarah P. Duke Gardens. Finally, when expansion came after World War II, growth centered along the perimeter of West Campus where the university owned ample land unrestricted by a grid of city streets. As a result, the architectural sense of order and repose on East Campus is reinforced today by a quietude that comes from being out of the mainstream.

Old Main

17. Old Main-Washington Duke Building
Samuel Leary, 1890–1892

The most imposing of the early buildings was Old Main, later designated
the Washington Duke Building. Designed by Samuel Leary of Philadelphia,
it was built of red brick in the Romanesque Revival style. Despite its brief
troubled life, it is fondly remembered as Old Main. It was begun in 1890.
The collapse of its central tower during construction delayed the opening of
classes on the new Durham site. Old Main contained classrooms, a chapel,
and administrative offices on the first floor, and sixty dormitory rooms on
the second and third floors. State of the art when it opened in 1892, it was
heated and had indoor plumbing. The trustees voted to demolish it in 1910;
shortly thereafter it burned, and its insurance provided the financially troubled college a brief respite.

18. Epworth Hall *1891–1892, architect unknown*

The College Inn was built in 1891–1892 and renamed Epworth in 1896. The
portion that survives is approximately one-third of the original building.
Designed by "a young Washington, D.C. architect" whose identity is
unknown, Epworth originally resembled a rambling resort hotel, with
porches, dormers, bay windows, towers, and turrets. Reveling in a variety
of materials, including wooden shingles, clapboards, stone, and turned
ornament, it was an architectural omelet. It is said to have cost $31,679.30.

Epworth Hall, circa 1890s

Epworth Hall, today

In the beginning, everything took place in Epworth. The dining room seated 250, and it had seventy-five dormitory rooms. The main wings were four stories high and contained classrooms, social rooms, a chapel, kitchen, and large lobby. Too large to be maintained efficiently, Epworth suffered the removal of two wings and its towers in 1914, leaving approximately half of the original dormitory rooms; other functions moved elsewhere. The present remnant is worth fixing in the author's mind's eye, for it is the architectural omelet of the university.

The Ark

19. The Ark *1898, architect unknown*

The Ark was built in 1898 as a gymnasium. It was given to Trinity by Benjamin N. Duke to honor his son, Angier B. Duke. The Ark may have been the first college gymnasium in North Carolina. In addition to its playing floor, it had an indoor track, swimming pool, bowling alley, and showers. The first scheduled "big four"—Duke, Wake Forest, UNC, and NC State—basketball game took place here on March 2, 1906. (Wake beat Duke 24 to 10.) When the Memorial Gymnasium was completed in 1923, the Ark came to serve a variety of tenants over the years. From 1923 through 1930 the college laundry occupied much of the Ark. In 1933 Sandals, a sorority, remodeled the first floor as a recreation hall. Since then it has been known as the Ark, an allusion to Noah's couples, for entry was made by a narrow gangplank-like wooden bridge. It is now a dance studio; its large windows and open interior—the two-story former gymnasium space—and resilient wooden frame and floor make it a favorite among dancers.

20. Crowell Science Building *1892, architect unknown*

John F. Crowell, who was president of Trinity from 1887 to 1894 and presided over the college's move to Durham, donated $8,000 to erect this building. He did so as a memorial to his wife, Laura Getz Crowell, who had died when they were newlyweds. Initially called the Technological Building, it housed the departments of chemistry, physics, biology, and engineering, a science museum, workshops, and a heating and generating plant that served other college buildings. President Crowell wanted to emphasize applied science, and "thus," writes William King, Duke University archivist, "the natural sciences became the only subject in the college curriculum to be taught in a building entirely their own." President Crowell resigned in 1894, and two years later the trustees renamed the building. Today the name *Crowell* connotes president Crowell, although this is not what he had in mind when he paid for the building.

Academic programs moved out of Crowell as the new campuses developed. The heating plant was shut down in 1927. The generating plant, already obsolete, had ceased operating in 1912. During the 1920s the upper floors were used for storage. In 1935, however, the building took on a new life as the Pan Hellenic Building, when the second and third floors were divided into ten sorority rooms. After World War II the first floor was renovated as a post office, store, and grill, and Crowell became an active social center. The University Press, which has since moved to Brightleaf Square, was housed here for a time. The offices of student development and housing assignments, a dance studio, and a community service center currently occupy Crowell.

Crowell Science Building

East Duke Building

21. East Duke and West Duke Buildings   *C.C. Hook, 1911–1912*

Even as dissatisfaction was growing with Old Main, new buildings were being erected behind it. C. C. Hook of Charlotte designed East Duke and West Duke, and Jarvis and Aycock residence halls. Individually and as a group, these four buildings possess a symmetry that hints at the future. Hook's proposals show he wanted to develop a coherent campus, for he suggested connecting the East and West buildings with an arcade and creating a pair of shelters flanking a pillared entrance to the campus on Main Street. Hook also designed a central bell tower as a focal point. None of

Proposed entrance for East Campus

these plans was executed. Nonetheless, President Few understood the importance of a sense of place and recommended to the trustees that they officially name the space framed by the four buildings *The Yard*, an allusion no doubt to Harvard Yard. Today the *Yard* is devoted to a traffic circle, but in 1912 it marked an historical turning point, for it was the first quadrangle on East Campus.

C. C. Hook, of the firm of Hook and Rogers of Charlotte, served as the principal architect of Trinity College from 1895 until 1925. The classical revival detailing of the East and West Duke buildings and the quiet dignity of their materials—pressed white brick, limestone trim, and slate roofs—suggests the ambiance Hook was aiming for before he was replaced by Horace Trumbauer in 1925. Today East Duke houses the department of art and art history, the offices of the president and vice president emeritus, women's studies, and the Nelson Music Room (201), an intimate and acoustically fine hall. West Duke contains the office of undergraduate scholars and fellows, Army ROTC, comparative area studies, education, the Kenan Ethics Program, the department of philosophy, student loans, and testing services.

East and West Duke, and behind them the Jarvis and Aycock residence halls (also designed by Hook), were still new and serviceable when the endowment made it possible to create a new campus. Today these four buildings stand out like a frontispiece related to but distinct from the body of the book that follows them.

22. Aycock and Jarvis Residence Halls *C.C. Hook, 1911–1912*

Aycock (1911) and Jarvis (1912) are the only Trinity College buildings fronting on any of the Duke University quadrangles. Both are named after governors of North Carolina, Charles B. Aycock and Thomas J. Jarvis, and both are built of the white pressed brick and limestone trim favored by their architect, C. C. Hook. Both buildings provide housing for 120 students in five sections divided by firewalls. The mirror-image symmetry of the four Trinity College buildings retained at the head of the new mall may have influenced the Trumbauer firm in its decision to create a setting that was exactly bilaterally symmetrical.

Near the East Duke building are several items which remind us that this area was once highly visible as the entrance to the college. Visitors often overlook the fountain, the cast-iron lamp post, the gazebo, and the statue of *The Sower,* for with the removal of Old Main and the development of the new campus the focal point has shifted to the interior of the mall.

Aycock and Jarvis Residence Halls, center

23. The Fountain *circa 1901*

The Fountain

Miss Ann Roney, sister-in-law of Washington Duke and maiden aunt of his sons, gave this fountain as part of a garden she funded to beautify the entrance to Trinity College. Miss Roney had helped to rear Washington Duke's children after her sister, Artelia Roney Duke, died in 1858. The four magnolias that shade the fountain are all that remain of the garden. Old photographs of Old Main, which feature the fountain and the magnolias, show that the entrance to Trinity was located about seventy yards east of the present entrance. Like Epworth, the fountain has been truncated over time. It originally had another tier, or basin, and a finial topped by a swan. Only the lower basin and pedestal remain.

24. Stagg Pavilion *1902, architect unknown*

Like The Fountain, Stagg Pavilion appears in early photographs as one of the ornaments adjacent to the main entrance to Trinity College. (The central tower and entry to Old Main was to the west of the Pavilion.) It was built in 1902 with funds donated by Mrs. James E. Stagg, daughter of Mary Duke Lyon, who in turn was Washington Duke's daughter. James E. Stagg was a Trinity trustee and a business associate of the Dukes.

Stagg Pavilion, with The Sower, *left*

The Sower

25. The Sower   *Stephan Anton Friedrich Walter, sculptor, circa 1890s*

This bronze statue by Stephan Anton Friedrich Walter, a nineteenth-century German sculptor, represents a seventeenth-century peasant sowing seeds. Like the paintings of Jean François Millet, *The Sower* evokes the nobility of toil and the biblical parable that we reap what we sow and must be mindful of the future. Originally located on James B. Duke's estate in Somerville, New Jersey, the statue was admired by Trinity president, John C. Kilgo, and James B. Duke gave it to the college in 1914.

26. Craven Memorial Lamppost *1905*

Craven Memorial Lamppost

When it was erected in 1905 this ornate cast-iron lamppost was the first outdoor light on campus. The class of 1905 donated the light in honor of Braxton Craven (1822–1882), who was president of Trinity College for forty years, 1842 to1882. The lamppost originally stood in front of Craven Memorial Hall, which served as a chapel, and this probably explains the religious allusion in the inscription likening the college to "a light which lighteth all men." Craven Memorial Hall was demolished to make way for the new Georgian buildings, and since then the lamppost has moved numerous times. It even spent time off campus, having been sent to surplus and subsequently sold to an antique dealer. It was tracked down in Philadelphia and installed here in 1990.

27. Washington Duke Statue *Edward V. Valentine, sculptor, 1905*

This bronze, seated figure of Washington Duke (1820–1905), by Richmond sculptor Edward V. Valentine, is placed near the site of Old Main, which was renamed the Washington Duke Building in 1896 in recognition of his contributions to the college. This apt placement of the statue recognizes Duke's role as one of the founders of Trinity College in Durham and as the patriarch of the Duke family. His son, James B. Duke, established the endowment to honor and extend the family philanthropic tradition begun by Washington Duke.

Washington Duke Statue

East Campus wall

28. The Wall *1915*

East Campus visitors often see joggers and power walkers circumnavigat-
ing the grounds on the 1.7-mile cinder track located just inside the wall.
Benjamin Newton Duke gave funds for the three-foot-high granite wall in
1915. Like the four buildings designed by C.C. Hook, the wall was part of the
early-twentieth-century growth of Trinity College. The jogging track was
developed in 1994 and is a reminder that a race track was an important feature of the fairgrounds that occupied the site given to the college by Julian
S. Carr. As a clear and rigid boundary, the wall is compatible with the obvious geometry of the 1925 Georgian campus it encloses.

Carr Building.

29. Carr Building *Office of Horace Trumbauer, 1927*

This building is named for Julian S. Carr, who donated the 62-acre East Campus site to Trinity College. Carr, a powerful rival of the Dukes in the tobacco business, served on Trinity's board before the college moved to Durham. In 1885, when the college was struggling financially, Carr made a gift of $10,000—the largest given by an individual up to that time—which started the Trinity College endowment. The Carr building was designed to contain twenty classrooms and twenty faculty offices. The university thoroughly renovated it in 1992; the history department is the principal tenant today.

30. Duke University Museum of Art
Office of Horace Trumbauer, 1927;
renovation, Carr, Harrison, Pruden & DePasquale, 1969

The academic building directly across the mall from the Carr Building was originally built as the Science Building, but since 1969 has mostly been occupied by the Duke University Museum of Art. The museum is open to the public (closed Mondays and holidays). Its varied permanent collections are excellent, and changing teaching exhibits present issues in the art world and explore how art history and criticism are formulated.

The museum entry demonstrates the efficacy of dramatic contrast as an architectural device. Outside we face the precisely framed Georgian style facade, but upon entering the lobby we are confronted with a free flying spiral staircase, a glass wall, and the cavernous void of a two-story gallery—the result of a 1969 transformation of the interior. Classrooms and

Duke Museum of Art

offices occupy the wings and more galleries are on the second floor. The permanent collections include old master paintings, the Brummer Collection of medieval and Renaissance art (especially notable for its sculpture), the Duke Collection focusing on the classical world (bronze age through the late Roman Empire), a significant collection of Russian art, and a nationally important collection of pre-Columbian art.

31. Wilson House, Giles House, Bassett House, and Brown House *Office of Horace Trumbauer, 1927*

Concerning the evocative power of old buildings, John Ruskin wrote that the "greatest glory of a building ... is in its Age, and in that deep sense of voicefulness, of stern watching, of mysterious sympathy, nay, even of approval or condemnation, which we feel in walls that have long been washed by the passing waves of humanity."

Wilson House and Giles House, both residential buildings, remind us of Washington Duke's commitment to admit women "on an equal footing with men," and James B. Duke's belief that Duke graduates would "uplift" mankind. Giles House was named in honor of three sisters—Mary, Persis, and Theresa Giles—who graduated from Trinity in 1878. They founded the Greenwood Female College in Greenwood, South Carolina, in 1885.

Wilson House is named in honor of Mary Grace Wilson, who retired as dean of undergraduate women in 1970, having worked in various roles at Duke for forty years.

Lilly Library

32. Lilly Library

Office of Horace Trumbauer, 1927; renovation, Haskin, Rice, Savage & Pearce, 1993

Until 1969 this building served the Woman's College as both library and art museum, a combination of functions reflecting the unstated assumption that women have an affinity for the arts. In 1993, when the building was

Lilly Library interior, the mural Three Faces of Femininity, *upper right*

renovated, a large mural titled *Three Faces of Femininity* by Irene Roderick was installed in the main reading room. The artist portrays strength, intelligence, and passion as feminine attributes, a forceful late-twentieth-century view of women's potential and role in society.

The library was designed to accommodate 225,000 volumes. Today it is linked electronically to the university-wide library system and the electronic internet world beyond. Visitors may find the computer-based study area (just inside the entry to the right) and the James A. Thomas reading room (on the second floor) interesting. Take time for a brief detour to go upstairs, as the balconies at either end of the main lobby offer a grand view through the building and provide access to the tranquil James A. Thomas Memorial Room. It occupies a rectangle along the upper floor with five arched windows overlooking the mall. Classical moldings, staid upholstered chairs and sofas, reading tables, and Chinese tapestries, urns, and intricately carved and inlaid furniture combine to create the atmosphere of an urbane clubroom. James Thomas, an associate of James B. Duke, introduced cigarettes to the Far East.

33. The Union

Office of Horace Trumbauer, 1927;
renovation, Thomas Riccas & Associates with Livermore Edwards & Associates, 1994

The Union is almost a mirror image of the library across the mall. Like the library, the interior of the Union was renovated in1994. Its oak-paneled, two-story lobby provides a spatial contrast to the contemporary food court in the center of the building. Here students can choose from a grill station, bakery, beverage bar, hot food line, deli, pizza station, or salad and fruit bar. There are spacious two-story dining halls on either side of the food court. One end of the dining hall on the left has been sub-divided with a glazed wall, which provides space for the Trinity Café, a coffee shop, without disturbing the sense of spaciousness. The main floor of the Union, like the lobby of the Duke University Museum of Art, represents a notable example of the successful adaptive reuse of an historic interior.

Food Court

East Campus dining hall

The basement of the Union contains a post office, convenience store, and rest rooms; the second story is occupied by informal meeting rooms.

Baldwin Auditorium and Benjamin N. Duke Statue

34. Baldwin Auditorium   *Office of Horace Trumbauer, 1927*

Alice Baldwin, with a Ph.D. from the University of Chicago, joined the Trinity faculty as an assistant professor of history in 1923. She later became the first woman faculty member at Duke, helped plan the Woman's College, and served as its first dean. Prior to her retirement in 1947, in addition to serving as an administrator, she published as an historian, was active in national professional organizations, and was appointed during World War II to the federal board that organized the Women's Auxiliary Volunteers (WAVES).

The fully equipped auditorium seats 1,400, and when the Woman's College was new, it was used as a chapel. Today it is used for large classes as well as for performances. Like other American university buildings inspired by the Pantheon, such as Thomas Jefferson's University of Virginia Library or McKim Mead & White's Low Library at Columbia University, the Baldwin Auditorium evokes a sense of permanence and resolution; it emphasizes the strong impact of the Georgian-style East Campus mall.

When Baldwin hosted frequent chapel services it must have held a more psychologically significant role on campus than it does today. Its principal importance today rests in its role as a visual focal point. Often locked and silent, it reinforces the sense of tranquility and quietude that characterizes the East Campus quadrangle.

35. Benjamin Newton Duke Statue   *Stephen H. Smith, sculptor, 1999*

This bronze statue by Stephen H. Smith of Charlotte was dedicated in 1999. Elected to the Trinity College board of trustees in 1889, Benjamin Newton Duke (1855–1929) was unremitting in his support for the college. His involvement in its growth and governance set an example for his more famous younger brother, James B. Duke.

36. Mary Duke Biddle (Music) Building
Edward Durell Stone, 1974

Mary Duke Biddle, daughter of Benjamin Newton Duke and granddaughter of Washington Duke, was a Trinity graduate (1907) and a major benefactor of both Trinity and Duke. For the building's dedication, Robert F. Durden, professor of history, wrote that Mary Duke Biddle "was always particularly interested in the aesthetic enrichment of the University. Her will, accordingly, stipulated that Duke University should receive not less than one-half of the income from the residuary estate administered by the Mary Duke Biddle Foundation, and the arts have been prime beneficiaries of this bequest."

The 48,000-square-foot building cost $3 million and was designed by noted modernist Edward Durell Stone in association with Holloway-Reeves, a Raleigh firm. Typical of much of Stone's work, it is elevated and isolated by a plinth-like plaza that serves as a base for an unbroken arcade

Mary Duke Biddle Music Building

Mary Duke Biddle Music Building

Mary Duke Biddle Music Building interior

capped by a projecting cornice and flat roofline. The arcade is made of brick with a white sand surface. White marble pavers cover the plaza. Neither the materials nor the design relates to the Georgian quadrangle or its surroundings. But in fairness to the designers, when it was planned there was talk of developing a new quadrangle using this as its focal point.

In 1958 a faculty committee had reported to the University Council that "in comparison with Universities with which Duke University likes to be compared, our facilities [for the arts] are embarrassingly inadequate." They recommended the creation of an Art Center so "the student in these subjects should feel that his subject is as much respected as any other in the University," and they noted the imbalance at Duke between the lack of support for the arts and the dramatic growth of the sciences. The renovation of the art museum and construction of the music building may reflect this concern.

The music building contains classrooms, offices, practice rooms, a library, and a student lounge. Architecturally speaking, two features are notable. First, the entry uses the strategy of spatial contrast also seen in the Duke University Art Museum on the quadrangle. In the music building the horizontal exterior gives way to a vertical, two-story open oval "well" in the lobby, and this void is made dramatic by having sky lights above and a fountain below. Secondly, although less obvious to the visitor, most of the studios, or practice rooms, have been tucked into the hillside on the lower level to dampen the sound.

37. Bivins Hall and Branson Hall

Bivins Hall   *1905, architect unknown*
Branson Hall   *1935, architect unknown*

In 1985 the university renovated these two buildings for theater and art, and it was hoped that proximity to the new music building would "draw together the creative and performing arts at Duke into something of an arts complex."

Funded by Benjamin Newton Duke, Bivins Hall was erected in 1905 for the Trinity Park School, a prep school modeled on academies in New England. The Trinity Park School played an important role in raising Trinity College's academic standards. When the school closed in 1922, Bivins (named for Joseph F. Bivins, first headmaster of the Trinity Park School) was used as a Trinity dormitory until 1927; it then became the temporary home of the botany, zoology, medicine, and psychology departments, pending their relocation to new quarters. In 1938 Civil Engineering moved into Bivins, and the testing of materials was conducted here until the art programs moved in.

Bivins Hall

The first Branson Hall, named in honor of William H. Branson, one of Trinity's early trustees, was built in 1899 as a dormitory for sixty students. It was paid for by Benjamin Newton Duke and first used by the Trinity Park School and then by Trinity College. It was demolished in 1935. The present building was built using salvaged materials.

Bivins Hall has the only example of paneled brickwork on East Campus. The Flemish gables here were echoed later on the Southgate

Branson Hall

dormitory of 1921. A portico with a flat roof was attached to Branson during
its renovation. These features notwithstanding, this corner of East Campus
is architecturally challenged. Buildings often portray the financial strength,
social status, or institutional influence of their occupants, and with this in
mind, Branson, Bivens, and the art studio building suggest the arts—except-
ing music—have been literally and metaphorically marginalized at Duke.

38. Southgate Residence Hall   *C. C. Hook, 1921*

Women attended Trinity as day students. In 1896 Washington Duke offered
the college $100,000, with the stipulation that before the end of 1897 it
would "open its doors to women, placing them in the future on an equal
footing with men, enabling them to enjoy all of the rights, privileges and
advantages of the college . . . otherwise, this offer shall be null and void."
The college promptly built a white frame house as a dormitory for female
students. Southgate, designed by C. C. Hook, was the first major building
constructed specifically to accommodate women. Costing approximately
$200,000, it provided dormitory space for 136 students in sixty-six suites
and contained dining facilities, classrooms, a gymnasium, an auditorium,
an infirmary, and apartments for the dean of women and the dining hall
matron. When it opened in 1921, 140 women were enrolled at Trinity, so
Southgate was almost large enough to house them all.

Hook designed Southgate to harmonize with the neutral tones of
the East and West Duke buildings and Jarvis and Aycock Halls, and he sited

Southgate Residence Hall

it to face Main Street—because when Southgate was built, the red brick Georgian quadrangle on the interior of the block still lay in the future.

James H. Southgate, for whom the building is named, was chairman of Trinity's board of trustees from 1896 until his death in 1916. As chairman, he is remembered for his defense of academic freedom during the Bassett Affair in 1903. As an orator and public personage, he is remembered for a brief foray into national politics as a vice presidential candidate for the Prohibition Party in 1896.

39. Gilbert-Addoms Residence Hall *Six Associates, 1957*

Gilbert-Addoms was built a quarter century after the Georgian style East Campus. It is a monument to the success of the women's college, for enrollment had outgrown the facilities on the quadrangle. Six Associates of Asheville designed the new dormitory to house 200 women; Gilbert-Addoms' special features include sun decks on the roof and a dining hall to seat 350. Designed to be architecturally compatible with Southgate, Gilbert-Addoms was one of the last buildings erected prior to attempts to relate new construction to the two historic campuses.

This residence hall was named in honor of two female professors. Katherine E. Gilbert, a professor of philosophy, taught at Duke from 1930 until 1952 and served as chair of the department of aesthetics, art, and music. Her peer and colleague, Ruth M. Addoms, was a professor of botany from 1930 until 1951.

Southgate Residence Hall (pages 79–80)

Alumni Memorial Gym

40. Alumni Memorial Gymnasium and Brodie Recreation Center

Alumni Memorial Gymnasium   *C. C. Hook, 1924*
Keith and Brenda Brodie Recreation Center addition
>   *Hastings Chivetta Architects with Architectural Resources, Cambridge, 1996*

The Alumni Memorial Gym is named in honor of the twenty-one Trinity students who died in World War I. When it opened in 1924, it replaced one of Trinity's oldest buildings—the Ark, 1898, on the other side of East Campus. The new gym was one of the last buildings built by the college before the endowment transformed the campus. Racquetball courts were added to the building in 1975, and in 1996 the Keith and Brenda Brodie Recreation Center, a 31,000-square-foot addition, opened. The Center contains a pool, an indoor track, basketball courts, and aerobics and weight rooms.

The relationship between the original portion of the gym and the new Brodie Center—a sharp contrast of colors and shapes—reflects a late-twentieth-century interest among architects in visual contradiction. We expect to find dissimilar elements juxtaposed on city streets, but we do not anticipate it on campus. The Brodie Center is named in honor of Keith Brodie and his wife Brenda. Dr. Brodie served as president of Duke from 1985 to 1993.

Randolph Dormitory

41. Blackwell and Randolph Dormitories

Little and Associates with Architectural Resources, Cambridge, 1994

The archway, or arcade, is a significant historical hallmark of both East and West campuses, and the designers of these dormitories used arches to suggest a contemporary quadrangle. The simplified and abstracted forms of the archways also allude to Georgian ornament. The architects employed gray glazed brick in the upper third of the wall to make the wall "blend into" the roof and make the buildings appear less massive.

At Duke things are often designed or named to evoke memories that reinforce a sense of institutional purpose. Both of these dormitories are named to commemorate places. Randolph refers to Randolph County, where Trinity was located before it moved to Durham in 1891–1892. Blackwell reminds us of Blackwell's Park, which occupied the East Campus site before Julian S. Carr gave it to the college.

42. Bishop's House *1911, architect unknown*

John C. Kilgo (1861–1922) resigned as president of Trinity College in 1910 when he was elected a bishop in the Methodist Church. The trustees valued his association with the college. They quickly built a house for him on campus and elected him both president emeritus and to the board of trustees; Kilgo became chairman of the board in 1917 following the death of James

H. Southgate. Kilgo lived here until 1915 when his travels for the church necessitated his move to Charlotte. The house has since served a variety of tenants. Today, like its neighbors on the historic eastern fringe of the campus, the Bishop's House is a quiet reminder of an earlier day.

Bishop's House

Athletics Campus

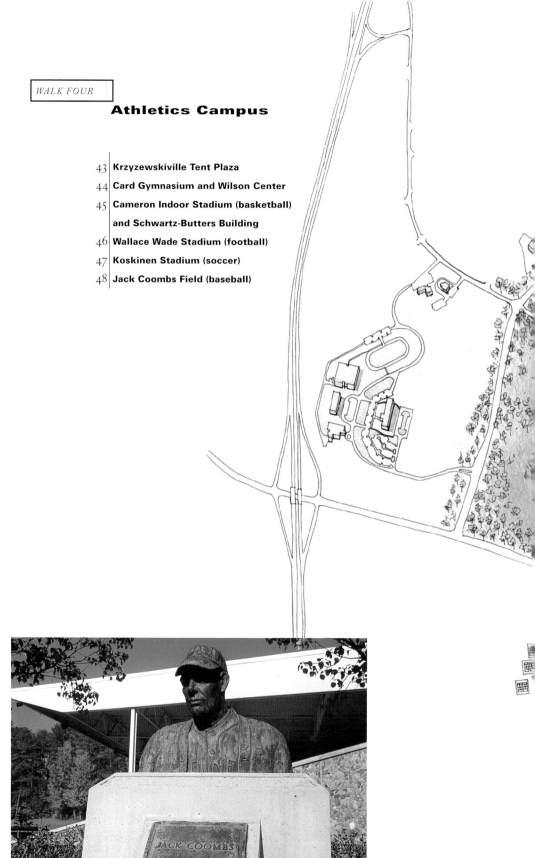

Athletics and Recreation

Plato advocated a balance of scholarship and athletic training. Athletics have been used for more than 2000 years to teach self-discipline, cooperation, persistence, and focused aggression—an array of socially desirable character traits. Spectators are moved too. Chanting, gyrating cheerleaders, a throbbing band, and roaring crowd, all create a visceral sense of unity. Now, with universities divided into groups based on academic discipline or class standing, athletic events often provide the most vivid moments relevant to the community as a whole.

Duke's major athletic facilities are contiguous, gathered into a precinct like the Elysian Fields. Clustered together at the west end of the West Campus ridge, they fit together like pieces of a puzzle. Cameron Indoor Stadium (basketball) is next door to the Card Gymnasium and the Wilson Center (aerobics, swimming, weight training), which is adjacent to the indoor and outdoor tennis courts. Wallace Wade Stadium (football) backs up to Cameron and is beside Koskinen Field (soccer), which in turn abuts the baseball diamond. Almost without exception, these facilities are screened or framed by trees. The trees give this part of campus an appropriately relaxed, open atmosphere; moreover, much of the construction nestles against the slope of the land, so the structures do not overwhelm the landscape.

43. Krzyzewskiville Tent Plaza (KTP)   *Cesar Pelli, 2000*

The new KTP Plaza is a successful integration of old and new elements—as suggested in the 1963 master plan—to create new quadrangles that extend

Krzyzewskiville Tent Plaza

Krzyzewskiville Tent Plaza

the pedestrian-oriented sense of place. The Trumbauer office had prepared plans in 1939 for the expansion of this area, devoted to recreation and athletics. Cesar Pelli updated these original plans in 1996. The new tennis building, the new Wilson Center connected to Card Gymnasium, and the Schwartz-Butters Building attached to Cameron Indoor Stadium form three sides of a quadrangle. The walks and walls, grass and lights establish sight lines and patterns that make us see the space as a whole. The effect is so cohesive that we are oblivious to the cars behind us—much as we forget or lose sight of the inland view when we are on the beach.

Some would argue that it is absurd to construct an elaborate entry on a utilitarian building, as has been done on the barn-like indoor tennis building. But this element should not be judged as an entry to the tennis center. Instead, it should be viewed as a theatrical backdrop on an architectural scale. It closes or defines the west end of the quadrangle like a visual parenthesis.

44. Card Gymnasium and Wilson Center

Card Gymnasium

Office of Horace Trumbauer, 1930; Carr, Harrison, Pruden and DePasquale, addition, 1970

Wilson Center   *Hastings & Chivetta with Cesar Pelli & Associates, 1999*

The gymnasium is named in honor of Wilbur Wade "Cap" Card, who directed physical education at Duke for forty-one years. He had an outstanding career as a student athlete at Trinity, loved it, and never left. Card organized the second intercollegiate basketball game in North Carolina in the Ark on East Campus, Trinity vs. Wake Forest, held on March 2, 1906. The historic core of Card consists of a playing floor (90 by 132 feet), showers, equipment rooms, offices, and classrooms. In 1970 a natatorium, designed by Carr, Harrison, Pruden and DePasquale of Durham, was added to the downhill, south side of Card. It includes an eight-lane swimming pool and a separate diving pool built to Olympic standards.

The Wilson Center, connected to Card, uses the visual vocabulary of Card and Cameron Indoor Stadium—metal-framed windows, Hillsborough stone, and a low tower—and recasts these traditional elements in a contemporary idiom. The open grid of beams atop Wilson's tower is especially suggestive.

45. Cameron Indoor Stadium and Schwartz-Butters Building

Cameron Indoor Stadium   *Office of Horace Trumbauer, 1939*
Schwartz-Butters Building   *Hastings & Chivetta with Cesar Pelli & Associates*

Cameron was named in 1972 to honor Edmund McCullough Cameron, who had then served Duke for forty-six years. He was head basketball coach from 1929 to 1942, head football coach from 1942 to 1945, and athletic director from 1942 and1945 and again from 1951 to 1972. Under his leadership Duke established a winning tradition. As a basketball coach, his record was 226-99, including three Southern Conference titles; in football his record was 25-11-1, again including three conference titles and a win in the 1945 Sugar Bowl. The Cameron Indoor Stadium seats 8,000.

The Schwartz-Butters Building, a new office tower linked to the west side of Cameron by a two-story wing, balances the tennis building and closes the plaza. The wing and tower, designed by Hastings & Chivetta with Cesar Pelli & Associates as design consultants, present a fugue-like repetition of forms and materials found throughout the plaza. The framing retaining walls and asymmetrical stairs and ramp of Hillsborough stone are especially effective. The low wing provides a concourse for Cameron, which

Cameron Indoor Stadium

doubles as a well-lit hall for the display of memorabilia; basketball locker rooms, showers, and weight facilities are below. The tower houses basketball offices and the student academic center for all athletic programs.

Sheffield Tennis Center, adjacet to Cameron Stadium and the Shwartz–Butters Building

Wallace Wade Stadium

46. Wallace Wade Stadium (football and track)

Office of Horace Trumbauer, 1929

The stadium is sited like the theater at Epidaurus—a classical amphitheater. Spectators may enter at the top of the horseshoe-shaped bowl and descend the tiers of seats toward the playing field below. The stadium seats 35,000, and is fringed by trees and open to the south with a view of practice fields and the forest beyond. It is an open, airy, and pleasant setting.

The urge to honor institutional history is especially evident in the athletic quadrant of the campus. The stadium is ringed with signs recording victorious seasons; more subtly, bronze busts of coaches and bronze tablets set in the slate border of the sidewalk around the northeast corner of the stadium commemorate the captains of each football team, beginning with W.A. Johnston, Trinity, 1888.

47. Koskinen Stadium (soccer)

The utilitarian, metal-frame bleachers and chainlink fence and the absence of any architectural embellishments signify that at Duke—as throughout America—soccer is still the new kid on the block. Practice and intramural fields flank Koskinen.

48. Jack Coombs Field (baseball) *1931, 1984*

The baseball field overlooks the towers of the Sanford Institute and a screen of mature pines and hardwoods. The covered bleachers behind home plate and the grassy slope along the first base line provide a sweeping view of the well-drained, natural turf diamond. The park was designed to resemble

Jack Coombs Field

historic Shibe Park in Philadelphia. The distance down the foul lines is 330 feet; it is 410 feet from home to dead center field. Jack Coombs, who established baseball at Duke, served as coach from 1929 to 1952 and had a record of 381 wins to 171 losses. During his twenty-four years, his teams won six Southern Conference championships, five state championships and won sixty-nine percent of their games.

Science Drive

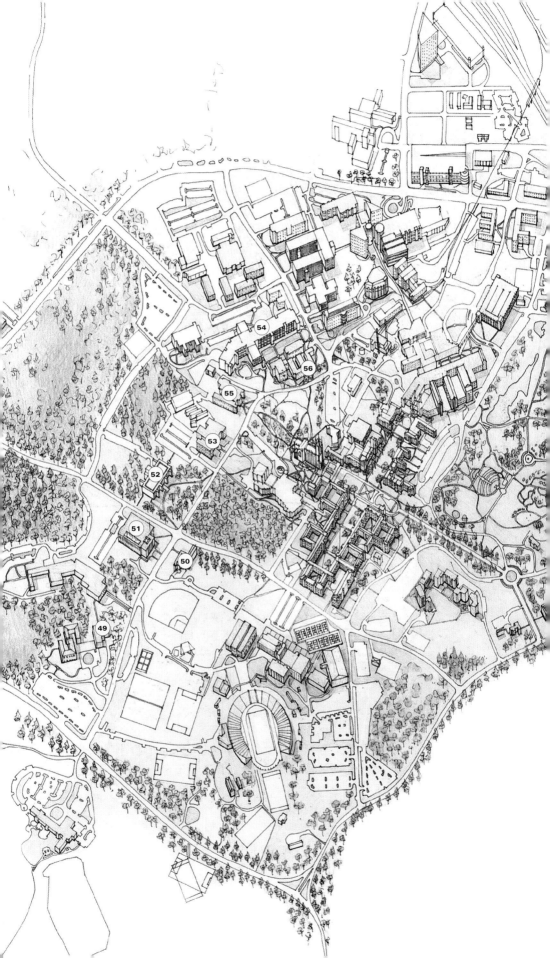

West Campus exudes tradition and gives the impression that Duke is mellowing tranquilly. This is an illusion. In fact, pressure for growth began as early as the late 1930s, when the original facilities were still new; since 1939 construction has been almost continuous.

Several early projects represented completion of the 1925–1930 historic core (the Chapel was finished in 1932, Cameron Indoor Stadium and the Few Quadrangle in 1939, Perkins Library was added to in 1948, and the Allen Administration Building, which matches the historic quadrangle, was not finished until 1954). But space in and adjacent to the quadrangles was finite; consequently the university administration asked the Olmsted Brothers for advice about expansion in 1945. The Olmsted Brothers prefaced their recommendations by noting that Duke officials "precluded at the very outset of our discussions the use of Gothic architecture for these buildings."

At that time a fringe of trees ringed the edge of West Campus along Towerview and Science Drive. These plantings were the result of C. F. Korstian's efforts. Korstian, who established the forestry program, had convinced the university to set aside a greenbelt in 1934 as an arboretum "free of all cutting or further molestation." The Olmsted firm believed these trees would create a visual buffer and prevent new construction from affecting the ambiance of West Campus. With this barrier in place, financially prudent, essentially functional buildings could presumably be erected along Science Drive. Engineering (1948), Law (1962), and Biological Sciences (1962), all built of red brick with limited or restrained colonial revival detailing were the result. They were sited at wide intervals along Science Drive to allow room for parking and expansion. Functionally these buildings were satisfactory, but they were widely criticized for being architecturally incompatible with the Gothic West Campus. In fairness to both the Olmsted firm and the Duke administration, "architectural context" and "historic preservation" did not become buzzwords until the mid 1960s. The greenbelt did not do the job, for a sense of place depends upon memory—the mind's eye—as well as sight lines, and the new buildings bore no resemblance to the historic campus.

Dissatisfaction with the postwar academic buildings and pressure to erect dormitories and more facilities for the sciences prompted the administration to retain the Houston firm of Caudill, Rowlett and Scott (CRS) to develop a master plan specifically addressing expansion, with the historic setting of West Campus in mind. This design study defined the critical visual characteristics of the old campus and suggested how to create similar effects using modern materials and techniques. CRS presented architectural guidelines, not specific prescriptions; they never suggested copying the buildings designed by the Trumbauer firm. The influence of the CRS study is evident in the appearance of most—but not all—of the buildings designed after 1963.

One aspect of the CRS report has been largely ignored. The consultants emphasized the quadrangles, viewing them as pedestrian-oriented, outdoor rooms, as a critical component in the character of the original campus. They pointed out that any expansion designed to accommodate automobiles would be fundamentally different. Science Road and Research Drive, instead of developing as clusters of buildings creating shared outdoor rooms, were developed as a series of isolated structures along the road—"beads on a string" was the metaphor used by CRS. While this new development pattern provided independence, vehicular access, and room for expansion, it also precluded a sense of community based on communal spaces. Visitors may find it interesting to compare the sense of place here with that of West Campus proper.

49. Fuqua School of Business and Thomas F Keller Center for MBA Education

Edward Larrabee Barnes, 1983; Perkins & Wiill, addition, 1999

The Fuqua School of Business, designed by Edward Larrabee Barnes of New York, is unabashedly modern. Viewed from Science Drive, most of its

Fuqua School of Business

sleek concrete mass is hidden by the slope of the land. Automobile access is from the rear, off Towerview Road, and the parking lot offers a view of its two wings splayed out dramatically from an open, hyphen-like connector which serves as an entry. The spacious, skylit corridor bisecting Fuqua's classroom wing is well conceived to encourage informal exchanges and spontaneous conversations before and after class. Designed as a common space, this hallway serves Fuqua as an indoor quadrangle.

The creation of the business school in 1970 brought together programs that had been scattered in at least five locations on the East and West campuses. The Fuqua complex serves three distinct groups: full-time MBA students, working executives who take classes part-time, and executives who attend non-degree conferences and symposia. The complex is large (over 140,000 square feet) and includes the R. David Thomas residential and educational center, which can host 113 conference participants, and contains dining facilities and a library, as well as classrooms and offices.

The business school is named for J. B. Fuqua whose gifts to the university now total $37 million, second only to James B. Duke.

50. Terry Sanford Institute of Public Policy

Architects Resources, Cambridge, Inc., 1994

The Sanford Institute exemplifies the independence or isolation of most of the buildings in this part of campus. Designed by Architects Resources,

Sanford Institute

Cambridge, Massachusetts, it is prominently sited at the corner of Towerview Road and Science Drive, framed against the hillside that borders the outfield of the baseball diamond. The design evokes the Gothic campus tradition by using familiar forms—a tower capped with finials, vertically proportioned windows, a steeply pitched roof, and contrasting materials. Here the Gothic limestone trim, which serves as a defining linear ornament on West Campus, is dramatically enlarged and dominates the design. Carved ornament—a source of pleasure on the older campus—is notably absent here; instead, the pattern created by the joints is used to express craftsmanship and the sturdy building-block character of the walls.

The lobby or commons at the core of the building is worth visiting. Named in honor of Joel L. Fleishman, founding director of the Institute, the commons is an adaptation of the interior of Frank Lloyd Wright's design for the Unity Temple. Like Wright's Temple interior, the institute commons is a gracious, open space rising to a ceiling of skylights framed by cherry ribbon molding and neo-Arts and Crafts style light fixtures.

Joel L. Fleishman commons

Terry Sanford was governor of North Carolina from 1961 to 1965, president of Duke from 1969 to 1985, and U.S. senator from North Carolina from 1986 to 1993. The institute contributes to the improvement of public policy by offering undergraduate and graduate programs, and by promoting research, publication, and professional training. Policy issues of interest to the faculty range from aging and AIDS to war and welfare reform. The institute seeks "to engage the world of public affairs by creating courses that directly address contemporary issues of public policy, by bringing to the campus leaders from the public, private and nonprofit sectors, and by actively participating in the work and thinking of organizations that contribute to public policy."

Law Building

51. Law Building   *Six Associates, 1962; Gunnar Birkets, addition, 1995*

The red brick part of the Law School, dedicated in 1963, contains about 100,000 square feet of space and was designed for a student body of 300 and a faculty of fifteen. Prior to moving into this building, Law occupied the segment of the main quadrangle next to Perkins Library. The symbolic wig and scales of justice can still be found above the entry there. Before its position on the quadrangle, Law outgrew first the East Duke building and then the Carr building, both on East Campus.

Behind the 1963 red brick part of the Law School is a four-story, 84,000-square-foot addition designed by Gunnar Birkets and Associates to accommodate 625 students and more than thirty full-time faculty members. Specialized aspects of this building include the library (encompassing 65,000 square feet and featuring movable shelving), computing facilities, courtrooms, and public spaces that encourage informal exchange. The addition is functional, but makes no bones about contrasting with the older building, so the visual effect is like an architectural prosthesis.

The dedication of the addition emphasized that the "architectural expression of the enhanced Law School building is an eclectic metamorphosis of the rich Gothic and Georgian traditions at Duke University."

52. Paul M. Gross Chemical Laboratory
J. N. Pease Associates, 1968

Despite its isolated siting, the chemistry building is a good example of the modern expression of Gothic components advocated in the CRS design study. The laboratory was designed by J. N. Pease Associates, with CRS as design consultants. It is very sculptural and visually active; eight towers made of aggregate panels of Hillsborough stone project from the perimeter and appear to carry the cast concrete upper floors. The exterior is based on the use of boldly defined contrasts—vertical against horizontal shapes, hard edged forms against areas of deep shadow, rough surfaces against smooth planes.

The interior reflects the special needs of the study of chemistry. The basement, for example, contains secure storage and emergency drainage for toxic solvents; here too are the emergency generators to maintain the ventilating system and lights in the event of a power failure. Machine shops, a glass blowing studio, and storage are also located in the basement. The first floor contains a large sunken lobby flanked by classrooms and the administrative offices. The upper floors are devoted to research laboratories for organic, inorganic, physical, analytical, and photochemical research.

The building is named for a distinguished chemist, Professor Paul M. Gross, a faculty member and administrator for forty-five years, chairman of the chemistry department for twenty-seven years, dean of the Graduate School of Arts and Sciences for five years, and vice president of education for eleven years.

Gross Chemistry Laboratory

53. Biological Sciences

Office of Horace Trumbauer, William O. Frank, W. Edward Frank, 1962

This prosaic red brick building—a straightforward stack of classrooms, laboratories, and offices—is not especially appealing, but the nearby bronze statue of the professor and camel catches the eye of every visitor. The statue, *Nature and the Scientist,* is by the English sculptor Jonathan Kingdon, and depicts Professor Knut Schmidt-Nielson, who was well known for his research on animal physiology. The statue reminds us that work done here in botany and zoology is intriguing and vital to the wellbeing of the world.

The greenhouses, located behind the building, are open to the public and are of interest to many visitors. Our word *paradise* comes from the Greek *paradeisos*, which stems from the Persian word for a walled garden. Many people find the greenhouses almost Eden-like in the balance of light, air, and moisture and in the emphasis on preserving, propagating, and understanding plants. The greenhouse entrance leads past work benches where labeling or potting may be in progress. You then pass into an area devoted to thematic exhibits, and finally into a series of rooms with climates suitable for different types of plants. The public cannot enter sections set aside for research, but there are extensive collections in the Tropical Conservatory, the Desert Plants room, the Mediterranean Greenhouse, the Fernery, the Epiphytic Room, the Carnivorous and Aquatic Plants section, and in a room showing plants that are economically important.

Nature and the Scientist, *Johnathan Kingdon, sculptor*

Biological Sciences

The geometry of exotic plants evokes the complexity of life. We are drawn to these patterns, fascinated by their variety just as we respond to the intricacies of Persian carpets depicting walled gardens.

54. Levine Science Research Center *Payette Associates, 1994*

In three respects the Levine Science Research Center (LSRC) differs significantly from the development pattern along Science Drive. First, located in a dell and partially screened by Physics and Engineering (drop-off and service access is from Research Drive), LSRC is typically approached on foot. Secondly, it was designed to house ten or twelve disciplines, instead of serving as an isolated setting for one tenant. And third, to encourage synergistic exchange among its occupants, the LSRC plan is unusually transparent and permeable. It was designed by Payette Associates of Boston, with George E. Marsh, Jr., as the chief designer. Large (341,000 square feet, the size of seven football fields) and complex, it may be the largest interdisciplinary teaching and research facility in the country. Academic units housed here include the Nicholas School of the Environment, the Centers for Engineering Research, Developmental, Cell and Molecular Biology, the Center for Macromolecular Structure, the Imaging Resource Facility, the Department of Molecular Cancer Biology, the Transgenic Research Facility, and the departments of Computer Science and Pharmacology. More than

Levine Science Research Center

any recent freestanding academic building at Duke, LSRC reflects the goal expressed by President Few in 1931 at the first graduation on the new campus:

> Everywhere in the University . . . we are trying to break down depart-
> mentalizing walls and make the subjects exist for the student and not
> the student for the subjects; that is, make the student the unit. The
> University is built and organized with a compactness that ought to
> make it natural for the students and teachers to think and work more
> and more from a common point of view rather than from the stand-
> point of conflicting interests.

Expressed when the campus was new, these hopes were re-affirmed—in fact almost reiterated—by president Nannerl O. Keohane at the 1994 dedication of LSRC when she said, "With this building, we breach the walls separating disciplines, allowing us to tackle more effectively complex problems such as cancer and environmental deterioration, which disregard neat traditional disciplinary boundaries." Furthermore, she described the building as a "metaphor in concrete, glass and steel for the future of sci-ence education and research in our country."

LSRC in its form evokes one side of the main quadrangle, for it is punctuated by projecting towers, provides sheltered passageways for pedestrians, and has a Union-like dining commons near the center of its plan. The clear division of its parts into discrete building-block-like forms diminishes the scale of the long facade, which might otherwise be overwhelming. Behind the commons, the Williams Hall of Science, a lobby-atrium, is accessible to the visitor and presents the meaning of the LSRC metaphor. It is open in all directions and crisscrossed by bridges and balconies on the upper levels. The lobby—like LSRC itself—is designed to encourage contact across disciplines.

Levine courtyard

55. Physics and Mathematics

Office of Horace Trumbauer, 1948; addition, A. G. Odell Jr., 1968

The staid-looking, red-brick Physics building houses the physics and mathematics departments and a Van de Graaff nuclear accelerator. In 1954 Duke, the University of North Carolina at Chapel Hill, and North Carolina State formed the Triangle Universities Nuclear Laboratory (TUNL) to encourage nuclear research without duplicating facilities. TUNL put up a separate building behind Physics in 1968, designed by A. G. Odell of Charlotte, which has received national recognition. Much of the TUNL equipment, including two large nuclear accelerators, is placed underground, heavily shielded by concrete beneath the building and parking lot. TUNL has enabled Duke faculty and graduate students to participate in and contribute to the development of the nuclear sciences. Dr. Charles H. Towns,

Physics and Mathematics

TUNL

Duke MA '37, shared the 1964 Nobel Prize in physics with two Russian scientists for work on the projection of microwaves and lasers, the projection of pure light waves.

56. Pratt School of Engineering

Office of Horace Trumbauer, 1948; Dennis Nicholson, renovation, 1982

Pratt School of Engineering

The history of Old Red (the affectionate nickname of the engineering building before it officially became Hudson Hall in 1992) demonstrates the practicality of the "beads on a string" siting pattern. In 1953 a 30,000-square-foot annex was added to the rear of the building, and in 1984 the 33,000-square-foot Nello L. Teer Engineering Library was added onto the west side.

When additions are needed, the staid symmetry of the colonial revival red brick buildings poses problems for designers who want to express contemporary times. At the Law School, this problem was partially avoided by adding onto the rear, but old Hudson Hall and the new Nello Teer wing are side by side and seen at the same time. The architects have used several strategies to make the juxtaposition harmonious. The massiveness of the new wing is obscured by the adroit use of setbacks and a plaza;

Pratt School of Engineering

its horizontal elements align with those of Hudson Hall, and its entry ramp, level with the sidewalk, makes pedestrians feel welcome.

Civil, electrical, and mechanical engineering are taught here, as are materials science and environmental and biomedical engineering. In addition to typical classrooms and offices, Hudson Hall contains various state-of-the-art testing equipment and experimental apparatus, including a wind tunnel, shock tube, and a triaxial press.

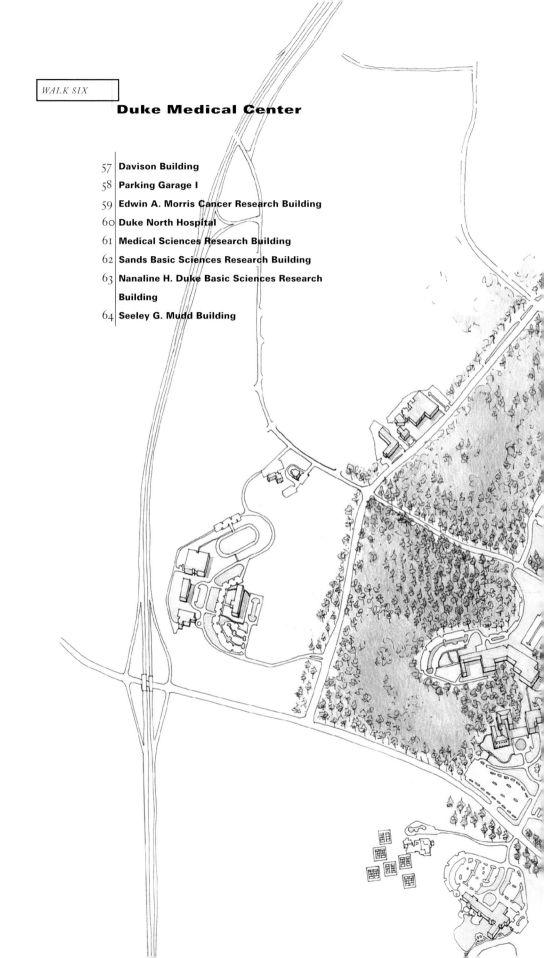

Duke Medical Center

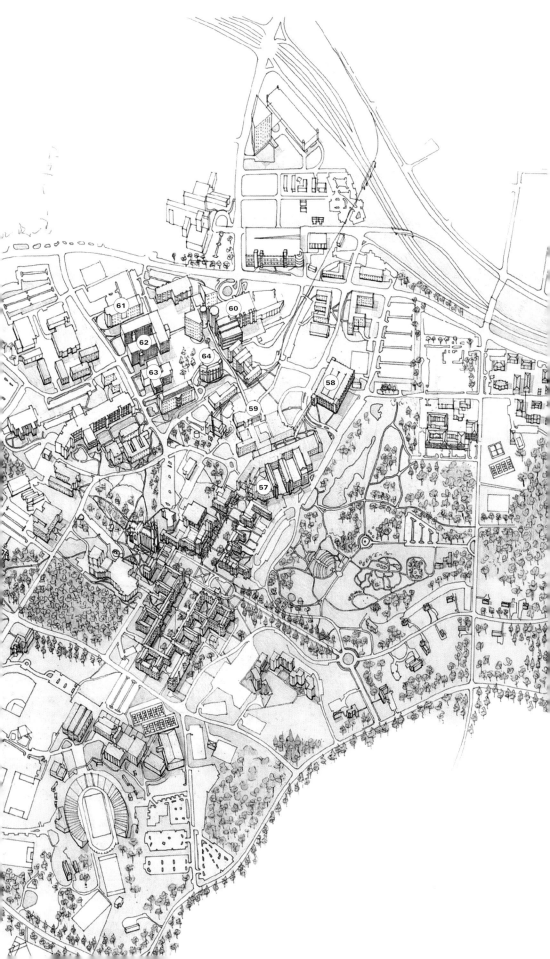

Davison Building entrance

Medical education, research, and service were part of the university's mission as defined by the Duke Endowment. In addition, James B. Duke's will provided $4 million specifically to create a medical school, hospital, and nurses' home. The Davison Building at the east end of the main quadrangle forms the original facade of the medical school, but it no longer serves as a principal entrance, for the medical facilities have expanded more dramatically than any other component of the 1930 university. Today the Medical Center consists of some thirty buildings covering approximately eighty-five acres and three million square feet of space. It occupies about forty-five percent of the university's building area. The Duke Medical Center is recognized around the world for its state-of-the-art research, teaching, and patient care.

57. Davison Building   *Horace Trumbauer, 1930*

Although few visitors enter Davison, it is architecturally and symbolically important. Its twin towers balance the Crowell Clock Tower at the opposite end of the main quadrangle. Davison resembles Rockefeller Hall at Bryn Mawr—one of the buildings noted in Frank Clyde Brown's scrapbook of architectural models for the new campus. The raised terrace that forms a forecourt framing Davison may be based on Haddon Hall, Derbyshire, England, a source cited by Trumbauer.

Davison Building

Shields on Davison's facade express the international nature of scientific knowledge and the world-class aspirations of the medical program at Duke. At the third floor, moving from left to right, we find: the Royal College of Surgeons, Edinburgh; the Medical College of South Carolina; University College, Durham, England; University of Virginia; University College Hospital, London; McGill University, Montreal; and St. Bartholomew's Hospital. On the fourth floor, again from left to right: the University of Padua; Trinity College Dublin; Jefferson Medical College, Philadelphia; the Royal College of Surgeons; and St. Thomas Hospital, London. Over the central entry is the seal of Guy's Hospital, London.

The first dean of the medical school, Dr. Wilburt C. Davison, a pediatrician, personified the qualities sought by James B. Duke and President Few. Educated at Princeton, Johns Hopkins, and then as a Rhodes Scholar at Oxford—where he studied under Sir William Osler—Davison had been teaching at Hopkins when he came to Duke in 1927 to organize the medical school. The original hospital, located directly behind Davison, had 416 beds. (The initial charge per bed per night ranged from three to nine dollars.) Additions to the original hospital, designed by Julian F. Abele and William O. Frank, surviving members of the Trumbauer firm, opened in 1940 and again in 1957. Unremitting pressure for growth necessitated a master plan, and in the early 1960s planning consultants Booz Allen and Hamilton suggested expanding northward toward the Veterans Administration Hospital, grouping research facilities along Research Drive, and keeping most medical education in Davison.

Today the complexity of the Medical Center is daunting. Its labyrinthine quality stems from the variety of services provided, the multiplicity of support systems and technologies required, and a history of growth by accretion in response to changes in medical practices, research goals, and patients' needs. The asymmetrical complexity of the buildings makes a sweeping view of the whole impossible; consequently, it is hard to get a sense of place here.

A good way to see the core of the Medical Center is to use Parking Garage I, and walk through the two-level pergola-connector to the Morris Building. The Morris Building, Davison, and its additions are now collectively known as Duke South of the Duke Clinics.) In the Morris Building lobby, go down one level and follow signs to the Rapid Transit or walkway to Duke North, also called the Duke University Hospital.

Parking Garage

58. Parking Garage I *Cooper, Robertson & Partners, 1996*

Cooper, Robertson & Partners of New York designed Parking Garage I with Hansen Lind Meyer. Like the Sanford Institute, it exemplifies the postmodern version of Gothic at Duke. Its exterior consists of simplified and abbreviated buttresses, finials, and aggregate panels, and the verticality and rhythms of these features evoke the Gothic just like verbal contractions convey meaning.

59. Edwin A. Morris Cancer Research Building
Middleton & McMillian, 1978

The Edwin A. Morris Cancer Research Building houses cancer clinics and research facilities on four levels. It is perhaps easiest to comprehend the Medical Center by imagining its core—the old Duke South Hospital, the Seeley Mudd building, Duke North Hospital (also called the Anlyan Tower in honor of Dr. William Anlyan, who was the administrative leader of the Medical Center from 1964 to 1988) and Parking Garages I and II—as five pearls on a string. In this analogy, the parking decks comprise the pearls on either end; the hospitals, with Duke North on the left providing primarily emergency and in-patient care, and Duke South on the right being devoted to out-patient clinics, frame the central pearl; and the central and smallest pearl is the Seeley Mudd Building, which contains a medical library and the Searle conference center. The "string" connecting these buildings consists

Personal Rapid Transit (PRT)

of an automated rapid transit system the Personal Rapid Transit, or PRT, and covered walkways and corridors. Flanking the core buildings are buildings devoted to research and specialized care, located along Research Drive.

One quarter of a mile separates the clinics, formerly Duke South, from the hospital, formerly Duke North. Clearly, something akin to a horizontal elevator was needed to facilitate movement between the two hospitals. Administrators considered the conveyor belt systems often used in airports as well as a variety of wheeled vehicles, but standard systems produce jostling and lurching potentially hazardous to patients and delicate equipment. The Otis Elevator Company developed the PRT to meet Duke's specifications. The fully automated cars can carry thirty passengers per trip. The PRT passage between Duke North and South takes less than two minutes, and the trip from Duke North to the Parking Garage takes less than one minute. More than 3,000 people use the PRT system each day, and most appear to take it in stride, never stopping to marvel at being whisked along on a cushion of air.

A rubber "skirt" frames the bottom of each car. Air forced into the space enclosed by the skirt levitates the car approximately three-eighths of an inch above the concrete guide-way. A metal strip imbedded in the guide-way makes contact with a linear induction electric motor beneath the car and causes the car to move along the track. The electric motors beneath the cars have no moving parts. The cars—riding on air—have no wheels; consequently, there is no mechanical vibration or noise. The cars can travel efficiently at speeds up to twenty-five miles per hour. There are 1,200 feet of dual-lane and 560 feet of single-lane guide-way, and each day the four cars travel a total of about 150 miles. The PRT system, which cost $6 million, provides a vital, secure, and efficient all-weather link between the two facilities.

From the PRT stop in Duke North, take an elevator up one level to the lobby, cross the lobby and step outside a moment for an overview of Duke North. The lobby emphasizes water (when the fountains are working) and light and intimately scaled sitting areas. Adjacent to the lobby is a gift shop, cafeteria, restrooms, and display cases, and for those who want to explore further, an information kiosk.

Hellmuth, Obata, and Kassabaum of St. Louis designed Duke North. Begun in 1975 and dedicated in 1981, its 750,000 square feet cost $94.5 million. Viewed from outside the principal entrance on Erwin Road, it is clearly composed of an assemblage of discrete parts. These different masses are joined logically, like a nineteenth-century cast-iron spiral stair; the cylindrical central tower is a vertical transportation core containing nine elevators, wiring, and plumbing. Five of the elevators are used by visitors and ambulatory patients; three are used for non-ambulatory patients; and one transports

Duke North Hospital lobby

Children's Health Center

supplies. The floors of what are essentially separate buildings fan out from the tower like steps on a spiral staircase. Floors to the right are devoted to patient recuperation and care. Floors to the left are equipped for active pro-cedures—surgery, radiology, cardiac care, and so forth. Much of the ground level is occupied by emergency facilities, the lobby, and administrative offices dealing with admission and discharge. Support systems for food, supplies, and engineering are located below ground like the roots of a tree.

Children's Health Center

By treating the exterior of each segment of Duke North as a distinct stylistic element, the architects succeeded in diminishing the scale of the whole. The main entrance is emphasized by a Mesa Verde-like overhang. This projection contains three large lecture halls: a 225-seat hall in the center flanked by halls seating 125 apiece on either side. Hillsborough stone is used at the base of Duke North and on its grounds, perhaps to suggest that these modern facilities sprang from historic roots. The stone, like the smell of Proust's cookies, is meant to conjure up memories and to reify the values that are Duke's foundations.

One of the most unusual aspects of Duke North is not visible to visitors: there is a full eight-foot space between floors for ductwork and wiring, facilitating mechanical changes as technologies evolve, without disrupting areas used by patients.

Adjoining Duke North is the new McGovern-Davison Children's Health Center, named in honor of Dr. John McGovern and Dean Davison. McGovern, a Houston philanthropist, Trinity, '43 and Duke Medical School '45, was a protégé and friend of Dean Davison. This new 900,000-square-foot center was designed by Kaplan, McLaughlin & Diaz and will accommodate 35,000 patients annually. Its exterior metal framing and tower contrasts dramatically with the masonry of Duke North and provides another interpretation of the Gothic in a contemporary idiom.

To see more of the Medical Center, instead of taking the PRT back, either walk approximately fifteen minutes on the elevated walkway that parallels the PRT track, or walk a longer forty-five-minute loop from the main entry of Duke North, west along Erwin Road past the Eye Center and the Medical Sciences Research Building, left on Research Drive by a series of buildings devoted to medical research; turn left again between the Bryan Neurobiology Building and proceed alongside the base of the Seeley G. Mudd Building and then up the stairs, which give access to the elevated walkway beside the PRT track.

This loop walk west of the hospitals covers the heart of the area set aside for medical research by the Booz-Allen-Hamilton master plan. It is a quiet precinct with few students and little public traffic. The buildings along the east side of Research Drive have achieved a neighborly harmony based on consistent siting—both in relationship to one another and to the street—a similar scale and landscaping, and the consistent use of concrete and Hillsborough stone. The best thing that can be said about the functional laboratories on the west side of Research Drive (Research Buildings I, II, III, IV, and the Vivarium) is that they are unobtrusive. Laboratories need, among other things, controlled access and tranquillity, so the absence of outdoor rooms and pedestrian bustle is explicable. The effect, as predicted by the 1963 CRS study, is an ambiance quite different from that of the historic quadrangles.

61. Medical Sciences Research Building

Payette Associates, 1992–1994

The Medical Science Research Building (MSRB), covering five stories and 190,000 square feet, is prominently sited at the uphill corner of Erwin Road and Research Drive. It is the visual flagship for the research buildings, which appear to fall into line behind it. MSRB was designed in 1992 by Payette Associates, Inc., and completed in 1994. They have successfully made sparing use of curved moldings, pitched roofs, and finial-like vent stacks—instead of Hillsborough stone—to evoke the old traditions. Costing 37.5 million dollars, MSRB is wholly devoted to medical research. Eighty laboratories and their support services are housed here, and researchers focus on making the latest biomedical research clinically available.

Medical Sciences Research Building

In 1972 Duke was designated as one of eighteen Comprehensive Cancer Research Centers in the nation. Scientists in the Medical Sciences Research Building and the Edwin L. Jones Cancer Research Building work to understand and develop ways to treat cancer and AIDS. When the Jones building, named in honor of Edwin L. Jones, Trinity Class of 1912 and Duke Trustee, opened in 1975 as the first home of the Cancer Research Center, its seventy-four laboratories doubled the capacity for cancer research at Duke.

62. Sands Basic Sciences Research Building

Perkins & Will, 1972

The A. H. Sands, Jr., Basic Sciences Research Building opened in 1972 and houses the division of cardiology. When James B. Duke was planning the endowment, he directed Alex Sands, his private secretary, to survey medical facilities in the southeast. Sand's report was instrumental in James B. Duke's decision to devote thirty-two percent of the income from the endowment to assist non-profit hospitals in the region. When Duke created the Duke Endowment in 1924, Sands, then thirty-three years old, became the youngest trustee; he served for twenty-nine years, until his death in 1960.

Sands Basic Research Building

63. Nanaline H. Duke Basic Sciences Research Building   *Perkins & Will, E. Todd Wheeler, 1968*

The Nanaline H. Duke Basic Sciences Research Building opened in 1968 as the first of the new state-of-the-art laboratories along the east side of Research Drive. It was funded in part by a $5 million bequest from Nanaline H. Duke, widow of James B. Duke. She died in 1962. Its four towers were designed to contain laboratories and equipment for the departments of bio-chemistry and genetics, physiology, and pharmacology. Support services and shops are located in a central core, and a library, conference room, and administrative offices are housed in a separate wing.

When Perkins & Will designed the facade, they interpreted the sug-gestions contained in the 1963 CRS design study and established the stan-dard for buildings along Research Drive.

Nanaline H. Duke Basic Sciences Research Building

The $26.5 million Joseph and Kathleen Bryan Research Building for Neurobiology opened in 1990 as one of ten federally-funded Alzheimer's Disease Research Centers. The building was made possible by a $10 million gift from Joseph Bryan, whose wife had been a victim of Alzheimer's. The Bryans had previously supported the construction of the new university union, the Eye Center, and an Alzheimer's research program. In addition to providing facilities for the Alzheimer's Disease Research Center, this building contains the department of neurobiology and the divisions of neuro-radiology and neuropharmacology.

At the dedication of this building Zaven S. Kachaturian, director of the Office of Alzheimer's Disease Research at the National Institute on Aging, commented on the importance of such facilities:

> All we have to do is look at history. If we look at islands of creativity in science and the arts, one has to look at places like Venice, Florence, Paris, Vienna, Athens and now Duke. They all flourished because there was a visionary patron of the arts and sciences. It's through such cooperation, through the creation of such an environment that I'm quite confident we will be able to conquer this disease [Alzheimer's].

James B. Duke and President Few would have agreed, for they too believed that setting, mission, and success were inextricably linked.

Seeley G. Mudd Building

The Seeley G. Mudd Building contains the Medical Library and Communications Center and, on the ground floor, the Searle Center for Continuing Education in the Health Sciences. It is strategically located between Duke North and Duke South, with direct access to both hospitals via the elevated walkway.

Designed by Warner, Burns, Toan and Lunde, with Danforth W. Toan as the principal architect and Yung Wang as design architect, this five-story, 50,000-square-foot building can accommodate 500 readers in the stacks, carrels, desks, and computer work stations on the upper three floors. Seminar rooms and an auditorium are equipped with modern instructional technologies. The Josiah C. Trent Room, which houses the History of Medicine collection, is especially notable. Like the rare book rooms in Perkins Library, the Trent Room offers a tranquil and inspiring sanctuary.

On the ground floor the 10,000-square-foot Searle Center for Continuing Education in the Health Sciences has five conference rooms, an auditorium, and flexible partitions that can be arranged to accommodate groups ranging from twenty to 400.

Washington Duke Inn and Primate Center

66

65

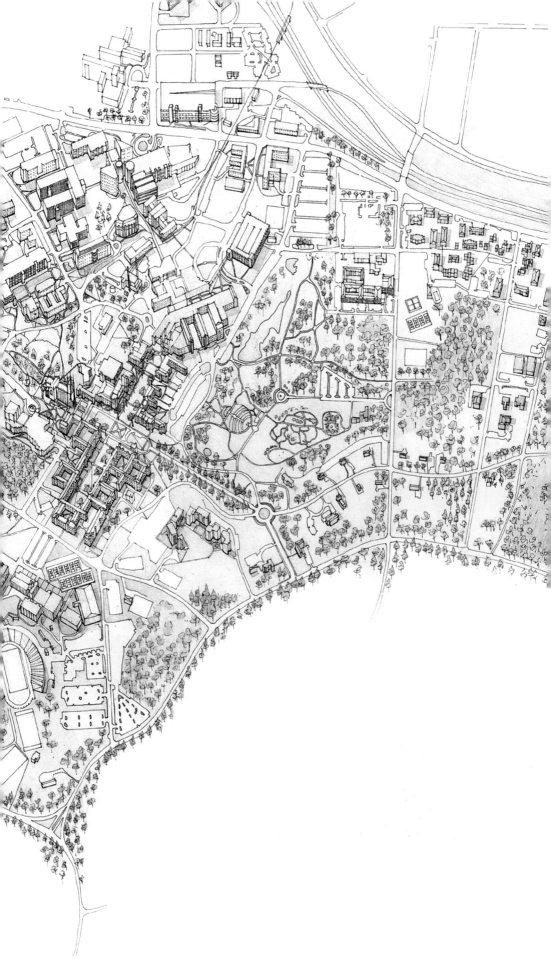

Washington Duke Inn

65. Washington Duke Inn and Golf Club *1988*

There are several reasons for visiting the Washington Duke Inn. The first, of course, is that the five-story hotel, completed in 1988, is a grand place to stay while visiting Duke. Secondly, for those interested in golf, the course adjacent to the hotel was designed by Robert Trent Jones and opened in 1957. In 1993–1994, Rees Jones, the son of the original designer, restored and redesigned the course, and it is recognized today as one of the premier courses in the country. It is scheduled to be the site of the National Collegiate & Amateur Association (NCAA) men's national championship in 2001. There is a good view down a fairway from the terrace directly behind the hotel lobby.

A third reason for visiting the Inn is the Duke family memorabilia displayed in public areas on the ground floor. At the end of the long hall to

Wooten desk owned by Washington Duke

the left of the entry is a Wooten's Patent Desk used by Washington Duke. Manufactured by William S. Wooten of Indianapolis between 1875 and 1884, this famous desk type represents the final flowering of Victorian business furniture before the appearance of stamped metal in the early twentieth century. With its many compartments and complex interior organization, the desk enables us to

Fairway from terrace of inn

imagine the mental and financial life of Washington Duke. An advertise-
ment for the Wooten Desk describes it:

> One hundred and ten compartments, all under one lock and key. A
> place for everything and everything in its place. Order Reigns Supreme.
> Confusion Avoided. Time Saved. Vexation Spared. With this Desk one
> absolutely has no excuse for slovenly habits in the disposal of numer-
> ous papers.... Every portion of the desk is immediately before the
> eye. Nothing in its line can exceed it in usefulness or beauty, and
> purchasers everywhere express themselves delighted with its mani-
> fold convenience.

Like Epworth Hall on Duke's East Campus, Washington Duke's desk
is a seminal artifact, a concrete piece of history associated with the origins
of Duke. And again like Epworth, the desk is in an out of the way corner, but
worth visiting if you enjoy history.

Bamboo lemur

66. Duke University Primate Center *1966*

At Duke there are places where the future seems to be simmering just below the surface. By contrast, the Primate Center evokes the deep, deep past. Knowledgeable volunteers guide approximately 12,000 visitors per year through the Center. (Reservations are necessary, call 919-489-3364, or visit www.duke.edu/web/primate). Located just inside the Duke Forest, a five minute drive from the Washington Duke Inn, the Center is devoted to under-

Diademed sifaka lemur

standing and preserving rare and endangered species of prosimians—primates that evolved millions of years before monkeys and apes. Seeing the lemurs, lorises, and galagos is an unforgettable experience, for their hands, eyes, and gestures strike an uncanny chord of familiarity. These animals have a "vocabulary" of fifteen to eighteen sounds with specific meanings.

The Center is widely recognized as a major force in the effort to save prosimians from extinction. Research here is based on what may well be the largest collection of prosimian fossils in the world (19,000 catalogued items) and one of the most comprehensive collections of living animals (317 individuals representing twenty-seven of the thirty-three known species). All of the center's research is "non-invasive"—that is, nothing is done that might hurt the animals, and the research supports the largest release program in the world. The center is working with the government of Madagascar to preserve habitat and increase the lemur population in the wild.

Like the historic campuses, the center's setting—some eighty acres divided between large fenced enclosures and smaller cages—is shaped to fulfill its mission. And like Duke as a whole, the Primate Center has established a worldwide reputation for teaching, research, and applying esoteric knowledge to down-to-earth problems.

Bibliography

Bishir, Catherine W., et. al. *Architects and Builders in North Carolina: A History of the Practice of Building.* Chapel Hill and London: The University of North Carolina Press, 1990.

Bishir, Catherine W. *North Carolina Architecture*. Chapel Hill and London: The University of North Carolina Press, published for the Historic Preservation Foundation of North Carolina, 1990.

Blackburn, William. *The Architecture of Duke University*. Durham, NC: Duke University Press, 1939.

Booher, Bridget. "Julian Abele, Mr. Duke's Architect." *Duke Magazine.* November 1963. Duke University Archives.

Durden, Robert F. *Duke Gardens through the Years*. Durham, NC: Sarah P. Duke Gardens, 1997.

Durden, Robert F. *The Launching of Duke University, 1924–1949*. Durham, NC and London: Duke University Press, 1993.

Jenkins, John Wilber. *James B. Duke, Master Builder*. New York: George H. Doran, 1927.

King, William E. "Architectural Firm of Horace Trumbauer." June 17, 1983, typescript memo to file. Duke University Archives.

———. *If Gargoyles Could Talk, Sketches of Duke University*. Durham, NC: Carolina Academic Press, 1997.

Porter, Earl W. *Trinity and Duke, 1892–1924: Foundations of Duke University.* Durham, NC: Duke University Press, 1964.

Steffek, Edwin F. *The Blomquist Garden of Native Plants of the The Sarah P. Duke Gardens: a Checklist of the Plants*. Durham, NC: Sarah P. Duke Gardens, 1997.

Much of the Duke campus was designed to evoke ideals. Its creators wanted the setting to inspire students, faculty, and "the institution itself." Subsequent generations have cared for and expanded the facilities, and everyone who enjoys or is moved by meaningful places is in their debt.

Current staff and administrators made my work here productive and pleasurable. The Duke University Archives, located on the third floor of Perkins Library, is the seat of institutional memory. The archivists preserve and make accessible information needed to make things meaningful, and I am especially grateful to William E. King, University Archivist, for his writings and for the conversations we had. Thomas F. Harkins, Associate Archivist, and R. Todd Crumley, Assistant Archivist, offered suggestions and provided documents and made me feel welcome. Readers benefit from the generosity of John Pearce, University Architect, who took time to conduct a tour of campus at the outset of this project. Others who shared special perspectives include William Louis Culberson and Richard A. White, who led me through the Sarah P. Duke Gardens; Joseph G. Pietrantoni, Associate Vice President, who unraveled the intricacies of housing and auxiliary services; John D. Manning, Jr., who showed me how the transportation system works; and Kenneth E. Glander, who introduced me to lemurs at the Duke University Primate Center, which he directs. I am also grateful for the hospitality of Richard and Emmy Scoville and Kent and Miriam Mullikin.

This guide is like a three-legged stool with text, photographs, and bird's-eye maps working together to support the presentation. It was a privilege to work with Robert Lautman, the photographer, and Jane Garvie, the mapmaker. Seeing things through their eyes clarified my vision, and I am grateful for their meticulous craftsmanship. Jan Cigliano, my editor at the Princeton Architectural Press, coordinated our work; with the composure of an experienced midwife, she made the process seem natural. I am grateful to the Press for giving me a chance to ruminate about campuses and, as always, especially grateful to Martha, Charlie, and Molly for helping with my ongoing off-campus education.

John M. Bryan
Columbia, South Carolina

Index

(*Italics* indicates a photograph.)